Travel As Transformation

Conquer the Limits of Culture to
Discover Your Own Identity

Gregory V. Diehl
Foreword by David J. Wright

Identity Publications
www.IdentityPublications.com

To inquire about having your book or course produced, published, or promoted, please email: contact@identitypublications.com

Ordering Information:
Special discounts are available on quantity purchases by corporations, associations, and others at the web address above.

Travel As Transformation/Gregory Diehl —3rd ed.
ISBN-13: 978-1-945884-24-5 (Identity Publications)
ISBN-10: 1-945884-24-X

Gregory V. Diehl
www.GregoryDiehl.net

David J. Wright, Globcal International
www.Globcal.net

Contents

For Anastasia, who gave me my final test of identity.

Foreword by David J. Wright

Human freedom and individuality from the perspective of a traveler is something that few people in the world ever truly realize or experience. I had not met very many of these people over the last 50+ years, that was until social media came around. Uniquely, the author of this book is one of these people who has traveled the world extensively enough that I can trust what he says about nomadism, offshore residency, citizenship, human rights and freedom.

Gregory Diehl is working on his third citizenship, is a United States expatriate, and actively maintains residency in multiple states. He has been around the block enough times in his young life to know what the world offers. The reader of this book can expect to learn things which I consider to be "outside of the box" or "off-the-grid." Many of them challenge our conventional understanding of who we are and who we can become. This is done by harnessing what I call a "non-state mentality," which is gained through building your international identity outside your place of birth.

Establishing your identity outside of your home country may not be convenient for everyone. They are already happy as North American, Australian or European citizens, which together account for 30% of the global population. For the author of this book and myself – who can both be considered to be part of the world's privileged minority as United States citizens – there are, however, further privileges that can only be understood by leaving. Perhaps you will experience some of the same benefits yourself just by reading this book.

The benefits I'm talking about go far beyond seeing exciting new places. Periodic travel as a tourist for a few weeks at a time along the well-beaten path will never give you all the understanding that is required to consider yourself at liberty in the world. Unless you are a millionaire, spend $100,000 or more per year on personal leisure, and travel at least several times per year, you probably don't see yourself in a position to make travel a major part of your life.

I first met with the author on Skype, as is the common mode of communication for people who may never be in the same part of the world at the same time, after he had already written this book. I knew then that I wanted to read it because it was a book that needed to be written and the world needed to read it. I was initially surprised, but I discovered we already ran in many of the same circles of acclaimed international travelers. After a few minutes, we both understood that we shared many personal interests, including global entrepreneurship and citizenship, and he asked me to contribute to his work. It is an opportunity of good timing for me. As a goodwill ambassador and observer of the Colombian peace process, representing an international NGO, I am getting ready to move my office to Bogota, Colombia from Caracas, Venezuela.

The information presented in the pages that follow may not empower you to begin living a nomadic life immediately, maybe because you do not know who you are yet. But Gregory's tale will, at the very least, teach you to see the world somehow differently from the way you did before. Perhaps you will start to see it as a nicer place than you have ever thought before; or, as Gregory will demonstrate, perhaps the very opposite.

From my perspective as a permanent traveler and expatriate, the book offers hundreds of possibilities to those who wish to adopt the non-state or global citizenship perspective. I am certain it will warrant readers who share Gregory's ideals to ply them until they can reach the crossroads and make a pivotal choice toward freedom, as many world travelers have already experienced.

Both the author and I understand that this, admittedly, somewhat extreme lifestyle is not for everyone. It is up to you, as the reader, to decide how much understanding you can manifest to define the limits of your horizons and what type of person you want to become. You can live someplace where others only dream of. More importantly, you can become someone you might have only dreamt of.

It took me over 40 years to realize my dream of living someday in the Guiana Highlands (a prehistoric landscape in Venezuela and Guyana). I first had this dream while studying geography at high school, but it was something that I had forgotten about by the time I was 19. After reaching many of the expected stops in life that were programmed into me, such as a being a responsible father, citizen, patriot, business owner, college graduate, and other things modern humans do, I finally came back to living in the Amazon rainforest. Here, I chartered an ecovillage and ecological project spanning 22 square kilometers, which I now manage.

My home here is a place we call Ekobius. It is my permanent legal residence, and where I am accepted as an honorary and functional member of the Piaroa tribe. The only thing that keeps me from residing there permanently is the current political situation between Venezuela and the United States. Because of the bilateral discrimination between the governments, I face many restrictions on my freedom of movement in my own home. But as a soon-to-be resident of Colombia, I will be able to move to and from the ecovillage more freely in the near future. That's just a small example of the influence that a person's national identity has over their ability to pursue their own dreams and highest identity.

With the help of a global team of goodwill ambassadors and volunteers, I operate Globcal International. We are an organization which aspires to offer the first legal alternative to state-based citizenship and identity in line with the (new) United Nations Bill of Human Rights for the 21st Century and other bodies of international law. By working with the existing international bodies of law, we believe this is the most viable path to helping every person on the planet to achieve the same level of respect and opportunities no matter where they were born.

Since the first edition of this book comes at such a critical time for human rights, migration, refugees, peace and globalization, I feel it will help others to find the inspiration to start finding the life they were always looking for. It will also help them to overcome their loathing fears of being alone in the world as an individual. The reader should know that people's very being and identity are based on their existence among others, and the perceptions that people have of them, which in today's populated world is often daunting. In reality, even when we are alone we exist because others see and interact with us and we keep them with us in our minds. How you appear to everyone else in the world is your own grand excursion in life. Everyone should make the most of this. The experience you pour into it and the risk you assume as a human being will determine your outcome and true identity.

Last year, I began a two-month overland journey from Mexico to Venezuela, crossing 18 border entry and exit checkpoints under irregular circumstances in most cases. It was one of the most memorable experiences in my life, with very enjoyable but challenging events throughout the journey. I think that if this book had been available at the time, I would probably have done better as an irregular traveler.

Since my trip over the last several months, we have been working on a global citizenship program that is accessible to all people, regardless of national origin, if they are considered qualified to possess a passport from their own nation. The program involves a supplemental passport credential (Laissez-Passer), open-source software, and individuals claiming their own identity, notwithstanding the nation-state, so they can work and travel as global non-state citizens to some 10,000 worldwide destinations under special conditions as contemporary travelers. The book you hold in your hands will become an essential part of our curriculum for participants.

The project we are developing has already made great progress with international law that is implicit over nations considered to be part of the international theater; but the wheels of politics are much slower than we can imagine, even at diplomatic levels. Fortunately, the progress we have made to date has avoided all of the mistakes our predecessors made in creating their invalid, blacklisted and unaccepted programs, which have all been declared illegal or outlawed by authorities like Interpol, the World Maritime Organization (WMO) and the International Civil Aviation Organization (ICAO). Fantasy travel documents like the World Service Authority passport (which is mentioned in the seventh chapter of this book) get more people arrested today than they enable others to cross borders.

I believe we are living in a world where organizations, corporations, and individuals are now the leading forces of truly globalized ideals. I am sure that Gregory Diehl's words will save many people, including myself, much time by increasing our understanding of international travel and our migration to places we want to go, as well as the people we want to be. I thoroughly recommend it as a part of your library.

Col. David J. Wright
Global Citizen, Traveler, Indigenous People's Advocate, and Ecologist
Founder, Globcal International

PROLOGUE

A tourist is one who carries their old culture to mitigate the jarring influence of new experiences.

To travel with a truly open mind is to forget who you were when you started.

It is to be constantly born anew and identify with ways you did not know others could exist.

What affirms you most?

What would it take to destroy you?

You grow in conditions that force you to think differently than before.

When you travel to a foreign place, do you experience this new life as your old self?

Or do you become a new self?

You do not have to pursue this path alone.

Exploratory barriers grow weaker all the time. Obstacles that conceal opportunities decline every day. People hear the call to start exploring, discovering a much larger world than they ever imagined. You are not the only one who seeks to answer life's inconvenient questions.

There is unconscious cooperation on a global scale. We improve our ability to trade and communicate, making life better for everyone by moving beyond local knowledge or limitations.

The process is thoroughly known.

The yearning to know more inspires many to depart from life's familiarity. Their pain stems from unanswered questions and things they couldn't yet think to ask. Explorers pursue new knowledge past the point of resistance. This is the labyrinth that all adventurers must walk.

Experience inspires new action. It is a timeless but malleable path to expand oneself through inquiry into the unknown.

Many fear discovering something awful.

There are deep and forbidden parts to each of us. They are the actions and ideas that we have been told were wrong to hold. What we fear about ourselves remains the same until we grow willing to confront it. Under broader cultural settings, these unexamined parts of us can become something more.

With travel comes the freedom to break away from what one has always known and explore, for the first time ever, what it is that makes one who they really are. It will challenge and test a person like nothing before.

It might be something incredible.

There's a part to each of us that has lived in us since birth. That part is the principle of who we are and can become. It is the instructions for how we respond to change and interact with the world around us and it defines everything we will turn into when circumstance allows. The past does not define anyone more than they allow it to.

What you consider sacred about your identity is only passing. It is your culture talking through you – a trap to stop you from growing. Each new perspective and unfamiliar stimulus provides more ingredients to make you grow.

You may think you will struggle.

The unfamiliar world is at first terror inducing. To venture forward into it is to survive outside your native environment. One's greatest fear is actualized when reality does not work in the manner they expect it to any longer. Without familiar limitations, one loses themselves to all.

The details of life will come and go. The rules of the game will be cycled and changed. You won't know what works for you until you see for yourself how different things can work.

You will successfully undo yourself.

What remains when you dismantle your familiar mind? Formative memories may be lost. You only think their structure is essential to your story. You don't have to continue living as the person you've always been. No one is their past or how they happened to have lived until now. They are all the ways they could ever be.

Everyone fears what they might become without familiar limitations. You will conquer that fear on your journey to know the world.

It's not what you do.

The goal is not adventure. Every exceptional moment on the journey is a distraction from the ongoing struggle of existence. The little, unexpected things can teach you so much more than the big, important memories.

There will always be a more novel experience to pursue and higher stakes on which to gamble. The journey ends when you realize that the answers can't be found that way.

It's what you discover inside.

No one finds their real self "out there" in the world. Freedom is not a target to chase or an object to pursue. Attention must be turned inward to the invisible restraints we all carry. This intangible distance is much harder the cross than the comparatively easy task of boarding a plane to a new part of the world.

If you begin the journey knowing that whatever is scary, difficult, and uncomfortable holds the key to progress, you cannot fail. You will eventually get where you need to be by changing yourself along the way.

This is not independence.

Independence means to thrive without attachment to the past. It is providing for yourself the things you have always needed the world to offer you. Real self-mastery is more than bending the world to your whim.

Traveling in isolation, you learn what it means to be alone in concept and actuality. You witness what you revert to when safety nets are stripped away and no one shows up to save you.

This is world resolution.

You cannot change what you are. You can only become more or less of what you are. The world cannot help but be affected by your growth. It will race behind you. It may admire or admonish you, but it cannot remain the same.

With a new identity, you make a new world to contain you. You will change things to how you need them to be by the standards you now hold for yourself. This is the path that awaits you when you have resolved your existence with the world.

This is your identity.

PART 1

The Ordinary World

Life So Far as You Know It

We all know the narrative. Someone who is bored or unhappy with themselves decides to leave their normal life behind for a predetermined time. They travel to an exotic location for a chance to explore a new angle of themselves and life – you know, like an adventure – and come back a changed person. Anyone who didn't study abroad in Europe or take a gap year to sleep in hostels around South America might have felt left out, that perhaps they missed an important developmental experience. Travel in one's youth is considered to be a modern milestone on the path to having lived a full and successful life.

I want you to stop thinking of travel this way. Do not put something so potentially powerful into such a convenient bubble. Travel satisfies that most basic curiosity to depart from regular life into something new, if only briefly, before returning to normality. By experiencing the way others live, we gain a deeper understanding of ourselves. Exploration helps us to question the boundaries that we were given to assess reality. It taps into an innate drive to discover what one does not already know and expand the overall awareness of what can be known. We can also turn that exploratory urge inward and challenge our internal landscape.

Traditional travel books show you how to follow the paths of those who came and went before you. They tell you where to go and at what time of year. They sell you the narrative of what a wonderful, worldly person you will become if you hike the mountains of Nepal, backpack through the rice paddies of Bali, or volunteer in a rural Kenyan village. There is an alternative. There is a holistic approach to global travel that will fundamentally change you as a person. I will show you, through both my personal experiences and the principles they demonstrate, what to expect as your perception evolves. You will begin to understand the world around you through the eyes of a new self. At the same time, you will learn practical tips and tools for living as a global citizen who sees the entire world as their home.

We all see the world through our own subjective lens, and this shapes our reality – our personal version of the truth. We use past experiences to understand every new observation as it happens, adding it to our cumulative interpretation of how the world works. Over time, we start to believe we have figured out an accurate model for reality. The more we encounter the same patterns of change, the less we adjust our schematic for the universe.

And then, suddenly, you witness something that breaks the game for you. Something occurs outside the structure you have worked so hard to build through a lifetime of experiences. It might seem like madness. But madness is just the mind's inability to reconcile its ideas with reality. People who know they are right remain blind to new truths they have yet to explore. They will suffer until a new equilibrium is achieved. Soon after I became a traveler, I came to feel ashamed for having had the limited understanding of things I did before. Travel showed me how arrogant I had been to think I understood my place in the world. Without the influence of travel, I could not have seen that the world I knew was just one of many possible worlds.

The ordinary world is the set of conditions that support your homeostasis. You forget about it like a fish forgets about water. You could remain forever comfortable there, except that you cannot prepare for every change to this system before it occurs. Stress is what happens when we cannot process changes fast enough. The older people get, the more structure they need to mitigate the stress of change. New things start to feel threatening. When big changes are sudden, like the loss of a loved one or another life-altering event, we must choose how to react to it. We can fight the change by attempting to uphold our ordinary existence through willpower. Or we can welcome the change and consciously adapt to life's new settings. The more open to change we are, the less difficult the transition will be.

Sometimes, the greatest changes aren't forced on us at all. Sometimes, we leave our ordinary worlds behind in search of more because we are have grown unsatisfied with what we know. The mind wanders from the confines of regular thinking, drifting far beyond reality's accepted rules. This is a self-initiated kind of stress. These people struggle to stay small enough for ordinary worlds to contain them. Growth is an exciting challenge. Curiosity calls them to do something greater – to become something more. The present moment is plagued by the awareness that there is more to see. There are still undiscovered ways to exist.

Most people are not ready to wake up from the established pathways of their life because conditioning locks them into a range of acceptable actions. Even traditional notions of counter-cultural behavior are part of the problem. When we deliberately try to be different, we look to the examples of the past and consider the lives of others before us. They've cleared the path so that we can be conventionally unconventional. True originality – or true dedication to self – requires the abandonment of all trodden paths. No one has lived your life before. No one knows what it means to be you. No one can understand all the things you will become when different parts of you are realized to their limits. Perspective is the mechanism for this change.

Explorers and innovators actively pursue discomfort. They rely on their ability to figure things out in the moment and readily change themselves. They cannot foresee every detail that will aid this process, only prepare their minds to watch for new information and adapt in response. They can do this because their curiosity is stronger than the fear they have acquired of losing the life they know. My ambition is to promote the critical growth of your own curiosity and the utter demise of your fear.

When you think about who you are, you can't help but also think of the world that shaped you. This version of you is just what you know about yourself so far, and yet you act as though it were the whole story. Learn to see your past as nothing more than a starting place – a launching pad to the enormous changes that await you when you are ready. Underneath these changes will be a common thread that unites them. That principle is your path – the real you that has been present since your earliest conscious moments and for each developmental milestone. These events don't have to conform to your culture's narrative. They don't ever have to stop.

Your ordinary world is how you see the universe fitting together and operating with fluidity as a non-contradictory machine. Everything happens for a reason, and it is your mind that interprets those reasons according to its working worldview and underlying definitions. Everything you call normal is subject to the limits of your awareness. When normal is no longer enough, you branch out according to the patterns you already know. You push yourself harder at the gym because that is familiar discomfort. You read books because your mind is hungry. These acts are necessary for continued growth but are nothing compared to the great unknown. That is where our expected rules for reality fall away completely.

When discomfort is applied, not just in a targeted way, but to the very nature of how the mind interprets things, a major awareness shift can happen. This accompanies the transition back into the world of inquiry you knew before you reached adulthood complacency. The allure of a controlled escape is powerful. Travel brings rapid change to our lives, but in a manner we can consciously direct. Each of us sets the limits for how long and how far we are willing to go into the non-ordinary. As soon as we surpass the exciting part of novelty and approach our breaking point, we can return to the ordinary. Regular life will always be waiting for you when you tire of expansion. It's the place you grew up, the people you know, and the daily tasks that create your perception of time. It is your mind's map of operating principles. It tells you who you are, what to do, and why you should care about anything at all.

When you travel to an unfamiliar land, you lose your unconscious bearings, and this challenges everything you consider normal about life. You are suddenly unsure of even the most basic things. The air might taste different. The people move in a strange manner. The sidewalks are thinner and the buildings are a different color. Everything is unordinary. Everything is important. Everything requires your sudden attention. These subtle changes affect your perception of your place within the new environment. That is why travelers often don't feel like they get out of the "tourist" state of mind until they have spent at least a few months in a new place. That is how long it takes the brain to accept the new rules as normal. To travel, your perception of reality must constantly evolve.

But when you've spent a while in one place, you will automatically learn and adapt. Once you learn to do things like the locals, you will reach a deeper state of identification with the conditions that shape human life in that microcosm of the world. This adaptation will fill you with self-confidence because you will know that you are not relegated to survival in just one narrow state. You will discover an inner strength you never had before and observe the world around you, changing yourself as needed, into the type of animal that is most appropriate for each environment. When the environment expands rapidly, so do you. You learn more. You become more.

Throughout this book, you're going to gain some of the skills necessary to analyze your life in a more modular way. You will begin to venture beyond the limits of the life you have always known. Culture pressures you to live according to a set plan. Instead, I am encouraging you to look at life as a buffet of endless alternatives. The only real limits are the principles of nature, not the imaginings of man. You are the only one who will have to live with the consequences of the life you have designed for yourself. You alone are the rule maker and scorekeeper.

Do not wait to adopt a mentality of change. Look for opportunities in the current patterns of your life. They are always there but take effort to recognize. The autonomous mind – the unconscious part of you that already knows how to get to work, or how the ground feels beneath your feet – cannot recognize anything outside of its routines. There is no way to categorize such massive change.

It is almost ten years since I left my childhood home in San Diego at 18 to explore our planet and in that time, the meaning of travel has changed for me. Travel is not about being extreme or unconventional like it was in the beginning. It is about exploring myself through the catalyst of new experiences. Through challenging my prior assumptions, travel became more than a break from monotony. It became the only source of constant acceleration to my personal growth. The chaotic path of those early years freed me from the confines of comfort. It shook me violently to my core, forcing me to see the things I had not been willing to accept about myself and the world. It can do the same for you. I can give you the guidance I never had – guidance that may have made my path more bearable in its darkest moments.

You must be willing to embark on your own path of deconstruction, discovery, and renewal. By making this bold choice, you are setting yourself up for a life that will be far more challenging, exciting, heartbreaking, and rewarding. It will be more of everything. It will be a life driven by passion, in service to the development of who you really are – whatever that ends up being. The alternative is to accept the restrictions that the rest of the world have already placed on you. It is to spend the rest of your life growing more limited in your options for active expression. You will live only by the script that your culture has allowed within its group paradigm. I hope the stories and lessons from my unconventional path will make this process at least a little easier for you.

No one else is on your path. No one else is living your identical life. Your starting conditions are your own. Your values and inclinations are yours. Your ultimate destination is you alone, isolated from the interference of the familiar.

PART 2

Call to Adventure

Introduction to the World of Inquiry

Every young person must enter a time of great questioning on the road to find themselves. However, once that door has been opened, there's no end to where it may lead. They may wonder if everything they've ever been told has been a lie or if the people who taught them how life works have only been pretending to know all along.

That was the troubling conclusion I would reach as I left my ordinary world to start on the path of inquiry. A life of international travel would be the tool through which I would seek answers to even the most basic truths of life. I had to discover with my own eyes how everything worked, no matter how far outside my familiarity I would need to go. There may be similar questions you've asked during times of radical change in your life when everything you once relied on seemed to fall away in an instant. Maybe you're in a state of great questioning now, which has brought your attention to travel. The seeds of inquiry are there and will sprout under the right conditions.

I lived out my childhood and teenage years as part of a mundane and ordinary Southern Californian existence. It was the default setting for my life, arrived at by the actions of people who came before me. People who spend their whole lives in one place like this tend to make huge assumptions about life outside their comfort walls. The bubble view of my San Diego County beach town was passed on to me by growing up there.

Throughout my childhood, the border to Mexico – a different country with its own people, language, and laws – was a mere 45-minute drive to the south of me. Like most other native San Diegans, I knew little about what lay across that imaginary line. Several years later, I would wind up living along Rosarito Beach, just south of the Mexican border town of Tijuana. I would drive back to San Diego weekly. The sudden change in temperament, cost of living, and culture every time I made the trip across the border gave me a new appreciation for the willful ignorance of my fellow Californians.

I, like the people I grew up with, understood only a minuscule amount about the outside world because there was no reason for me to learn. After all, everything I needed was provided on an upper-middle-class suburban platter. This made me overly self-assured in my sense of how the world worked. Truthfully, I didn't even understand yet how I worked. Underneath that exterior of a cushioned upbringing was a desire to question the worldview I had been given. A fundamental curiosity stirred within me to witness more of reality with my own eyes. Choosing to act on that curiosity has made all the difference.

Upon reaching legal adulthood, I began a journey of exploration over myself and the world around me. I had the good fortune of inheriting a small sum that gave me the comfort to assess many lifestyle options without the pressure to act. Because of my rebellious nature, I lacked the same mental boundaries other recent adults had about what to do with their newfound freedom. Before the desire to travel, I had been living on my own in a 1989 Ford Econoline van with a raised roof. It was the quickest means to get out from under the stifling watch of my parents and begin living on my own terms. Now my days in the van were ending. It was time to expand myself onto a larger playing field.

Nearly every authority figure in my life attempted to bully me into going to college right after high school. While I didn't know much at the time, I knew enough to be sure that was not where my ambition resided. I chose a different path, one based on impulse and passion. Many would consider my choices at this point in my life to be reckless or shortsighted. They would be right. But at the core of these choices was a calling to point my life toward the fulfillment of the potential I suspected I had.

I had never traveled internationally before and didn't even have any strong interest in doing so. But when the opportunity to visit a friend in Central America appeared, I saw my next major outlet for expression. In short order, I boarded a plane to Costa Rica with no Spanish language skills, no knowledge of the local culture, and no return ticket. I did not even know enough to be afraid of what would be waiting for me when I landed or the overall impact that my actions might have on the course of my life. My choices were spurred out of desperation for more than what I had at home. My destination could have been almost anywhere. I wasn't taking a "gap year" or running away from the responsibility of life. I was opening a door to more information about reality, having little idea of where it would take me.

The next nine months of my life abroad in Costa Rica were a period of aimless lucidity. I lived, for the first time since childhood, without an obligation to act toward any specific end. I had no familiar social influences to direct my behavior. The countless limitations I perceived under my familiar settings of home were gone. With the unconscious cap removed, I experimented with new ways to think and act, like a Californian teenager experiments with drugs.

Most mornings, I stayed in bed for hours, listening half-intently to the sounds of new species of tropical wildlife I had never known before. All my senses seemed more in tune with my environment, like those of a young child seeing things for the first time. Costa Rican coffee lingers in my memory banks as a completely relivable experience: a total biochemical association in my reference map of reality. It serves to remind me of how good things can be (at least, regarding the experience we call coffee).

I took extended moments each day to appreciate the vibrant colors of impossible plants around me. Ordinary fruits grew to epic proportions in the fertile jungle settings. Exotic foods grew in my backyard and filled the neighboring outdoor markets. I filled my days doing only whatever I felt like in any given moment. Each new variation upon once familiar things stimulated me further. I began to understand, vividly and viscerally, there was more to life than the things I knew back home.

With a heightened sense of ownership over my time, I taught myself new things I had never cared for. My appreciation for art and culture blossomed. I discovered old classical music compilations and fell in love with *La Fille Aux Cheveux de Lin*, or *The Girl with the Flaxen Hair*, by the 19th-century French impressionist composer Claude Debussy. I had always enjoyed popular film scores for their ability to tell a story with sound alone. Debussy's music painted pictures in a similar manner, but he did it a century ahead of his time. It showed me a new side to orchestra beyond the overplayed movements everyone thinks of whenever someone mentions classical music. It gave me a greater appreciation for the works of people from parts of history before my own.

My next awakening was that of scientific inquiry. During extended reading sessions, I chanced upon two hardcover tomes: *The Intelligent Man's Guide to Science, Volumes 1 & 2*, by the illustrious Isaac Asimov. They would prove to be among the most important intellectual influences in my life. I had torn through many of Asimov's short science fiction stories during the previous year, but I had not known he was also a legitimate, credentialed, and respected scientist. I marveled at his talent for bringing cutting-edge scientific principles into his fiction. He had a knack for explaining difficult concepts in ways that made sense within the narrative, encouraging readers to learn about the principles he described.

Discovering Asimov's non-fiction work during this phase of my life started an intellectual restructuring in me. Asimov shared personal accounts of how the greatest minds of our species had realized fundamental truths about the universe. His approach to education was orderly, showing the chronology of concepts as one important discovery paved the way for another. To make sense of complex living organisms, one must first understand the specialized cells that compose them. His explanation of complex molecules rested on prior explanations of simple atoms and fundamental physical forces.

Before Asimov, no one had ever shown me how human beings had come to know so much about our universe, or how every bit of scientific knowledge stitched so fluidly into all the others. I finally understood that all knowledge was part of an interconnected map of reason, stretching from very simple to cosmically large claims about reality. This integrated way of thinking gave me confidence in my analytical mind to arrive at solutions to the everyday problems of life. So long as I could categorize new experiences consistently and check them for accuracy, I could keep my intellectual evolution going at an accelerating pace.

I came to live with a man with an incredibly storied background. For the purposes of his influence here, I will refer to him as Swami, as that is how he referred to himself in a tongue-in-cheek manner. Swami had spent over a decade in India as a bodyguard to Osho (the infamous "spiritual incorrect mystic") during his rapid rise to popularity in the West. Afterward, Swami packed his boat and sailed out to an island near Canada where he spent the next seven years alone, tending only to his immediate biological needs. Swami had many stories and I was envious of his fearless independence and the 40-year head start he held over me.

Swami was the first person I ever heard talk about traditional spiritual concepts in a non-dogmatic and non-arbitrary way. Everything he taught could all be grounded in an individual's personal experience of any given moment. It didn't require one to study the history of any ancient religion, follow in the footsteps of any particular guru, or master any esoteric practices. His words were based on the concept of concepts, something the logician in me appreciated. Concepts were my domain. They were tools I could use. It showed me that an individual's greatest asset on the path to knowing himself could be what many spiritual sects warned against. The rational mind and the ego were not enemies to the authentic self. They were valuable allies.

With new understandings of art, science, and spirituality budding within me, I was ready to begin the most rapid personal expansion of my life. This would never have been possible had I not removed myself from my ordinary environment. When my old rules for life didn't matter anymore, I was free to choose my own path. I could explore what the vital parts of my identity were when context was stripped away.

To further the development of my new self and the erasure of the old, I would pack a small backpack and trek into the jungle away from people for days at a time. I wanted to see what I would become when even the most basic security was torn away, so I walked in a straight line until I grew tired, building myself a small shelter for the night out of fallen wood, palm leaves, and parachute cord. This helped me remove any distraction from my experience of myself. The inquirer in me had to see what I would become when there was no reason to consider the expectations of other people. What I found was that my thought processes slowed dramatically. Each day, I was losing a little bit more of myself, still unsure of what would replace it.

Soon, I came into contact with the indigenous Bribri tribe that populate the Talamanca region of Costa Rica near the Panamanian border. They invited me to stay with them at their reserve for a few weeks, which required me to take a lengthy canoe ride into the jungle to reach it. The tribe spoke no English, and I was still getting my bearings in Spanish. It was a lifestyle challenge I had been slowly preparing for. The Bribri lived in raised bamboo shacks, growing and harvesting bananas and cacao for personal use and commerce. It was fascinating to witness how these people had maintained their culture away from mainstream society. Despite the world changing all around them, they had retained their cultural identity in their language, values, and lifestyle.

In Costa Rica, I allowed myself to fill a much larger space. It was a new set of boundary conditions from which I could explore the principle of my identity. I was free to think about what I really wanted to do with my time, based on my genuine values. True freedom of choice such as this is a luxury most people never get. They follow the most familiar path, ever unwilling to deal with the discomfort of change. They get lost in the momentum of ordinary worlds. They cease to be who they are and become a response to the demands of their environment.

When I returned to California almost a year after leaving, I stumbled headfirst into dissonance and personal misery. The new attributes I had acquired during my time abroad were incompatible with the limitations of life back home. I experienced what travelers call reverse culture shock: the sudden inability to adapt to familiar circumstances. Family, friends, and even the first woman I had ever loved all interacted with the new me under the pretenses of the old me. To them, I was not someone who had spent the last nine months discovering myself. I had taken an extended vacation in a popular tourist destination and avoided the necessities of the real world. It was time for me to come back down to Earth and live by their standards.

I went from feeling more alive and authentic than ever to complete abandonment in the social settings I had grown up in. I understood why the adventurer cannot ever go home again. They change, but everything around them stays the same. The person I had spent most of my life being was not even real. He was just a character in countless personal narratives. Everyone in my life was the author of elaborate stories about contorted versions of me to fit their worldview. Without constant reinforcement, I had become something that no longer worked in their stories.

My journey into the deep had begun. There was nowhere left to go but still further down the path of inquiry, exploring the unknown within and around me. Everything that comes next in my story was only possible because of that initial leap I took into the unknown at such a critical point in my development. Had I stayed in California under the umbrella of convenience, it's doubtful that I would ever have examined my identity in the powerful ways that the last decade has allowed for.

The energy of an active mind has to go somewhere, or it festers and turns destructive. It is likely that I would have grown into an increasingly more frustrated person had I not been provided with an outlet to pursue my ambition. I would have grown resentful of life, blaming society for my failure to harness my potential. That is why it was so important for me to learn independence and adaptability at the time I did. I wish circumstances had compelled me onto a similar path at age 12 or 13 instead of 18. I could have made something more useful out of my squandered teenage years. Now, I was set to make up for lost time. I needed new data about the world, to see what else I could become as I purged my past and embraced greater challenges. There was no other pursuit but travel that would carry the same depth and rapidity of growth. I became obsessed with exploring increasingly uncomfortable situations. A door was open I could not shut.

The older one grows, the more difficult it is to take that first crucial step away from the conventions of our culture. The advancement of the mind slows as we age. Rules that didn't make inherent sense as children root themselves and we become the progenitors of these limiting ideas for future generations. It didn't have to be Costa Rica. It could have been anywhere away from what I already knew. I just had to be brave enough to say yes when the opportunity arrived.

There are countless travel bloggers today who encourage their readers to quit their jobs, sell their homes, and abandon their lives to live as they do. I'm not going to tell you to do that. I couldn't possibly understand your reasons for creating the life you have. Nor could I make it my place to tell you that what was necessary for me is necessary for you. What I do know is change must start somewhere. It is a far more pleasant experience to be the instigator of change than to have it forced upon you through outside misfortune.

Just as Asimov's guide to science taught me a new way to structure knowledge, you too will learn a new way to structure the components of your life. It all starts with a choice to open the door to rapid growth. For me, it was getting on a literal plane. Find out what the plane is in the context of your circumstances. When the vehicle that will bring you where you need to go shows up, be courageous enough to buy the ticket and start your journey into the unfamiliar.

PART 3

Departure from the Known

Embracing the Unfamiliar

It has been ten years since I rebooted my life by leaving my known world for a lifestyle experiment abroad in Costa Rica. Back then, I traveled with the perspective of a native Californian seeing the world with novel eyes. I carried my culture with me as my only point of perspective through which to interpret what I experienced. Now, I travel in a shroud of the unknown. Because I have no home, each place has the potential to be my home in equal measure.

Almost a decade of worldwide adventures has given me a diversified library of experience to draw from, as I make sense of each new place. I have changed along the way, molding slowly into the type of person who can go from place to place and solve problems in the moment, as required. I don't feel as though I retain a comfortable self long enough for it to be severely challenged by any oddity or atrocity. I know only the principle that guides my actions and leads me further each day into new experiences.

I write to you from the foothills of the Atlas Mountains, the tallest mountain range in North Africa. The elevation serves as an escape from the sweltering August heat and old city bustle of Marrakesh, a major tourist hub here in Morocco. I visited Morocco for the first time a year and a half ago, touching down in the more modern coastal city of Casablanca to see a young Moroccan woman I had met online. At that time, my motivation to visit the country was to explore the romantic potential I foresaw with her, despite our vast cultural differences. She was Muslim; I am secular. She grew up in a world that restricts the basic freedoms of women; I built my identity on the principle of absolute exploration. It was an interesting mix, for a time, which proved to be unsustainable.

Last month, I crossed into my 44th country via plane, from Berlin to Brussels. Although I crossed into Belgium from Germany, I do not feel I can include Germany on my list of visited countries. I arrived at Berlin airport on an overnight bus from Katowice, Poland. I have not set foot in Germany anywhere outside the airport. It is, by all practical measures, just a layover on the way to my actual destination. I have no real experience of the place. Belgium was the final stop on a phase of travel I started the month prior in Kiev,

Ukraine. After Ukraine, I made my way up through Minsk (Belarus), took a train eastward across the Russian border to Moscow, north to St. Petersburg, and then crossed over into Europe's Schengen Zone by heading back westward toward Tallinn (Estonia). I'm ready to settle in one place for a while now.

The Schengen Area is a group of European countries, cornered by Iceland, Portugal, Finland, and Greece (but not including the UK, Ireland, or Croatia) that share an open border policy. Citizens of any Schengen country do not need to have their passports stamped to travel to any other Schengen country. For a non-Schengen citizen like me, that means I only need to have my passport stamped once upon entering the zone and then again upon leaving, even if I leave from a different country. As an American, I am allotted 90 visa-free days every six months as a tourist within the zone, regardless of where I spend those days. For every three months in, I must spend three months out before returning. So, if I were to spend a summer in Italy, I would have to wait a whole season somewhere outside the Schengen Area before being able to return to Slovenia or Switzerland, for example. Complicated visa logistics such as these are some of the things I have to keep in mind, living the nomadic life I do.

After Tallinn, I took buses southward, stopping for a couple of days at a time in Riga (capital of Latvia) and Vilnius (capital of Lithuania), before heading to Warsaw, Poland. Buses are usually the cheapest way to get around by land anywhere in the world. In small developing nations, one can take a bus for only a few dollars to get from one end of a country to the other. European buses may cost more, but are more comfortable and often offer onboard Wi-Fi, allowing me to get some work done on the ride. When I travel quickly to new places like this, I'm looking for something anomalous and notable to make them stand out. Aside from the silent greenery in the areas outside of Tallinn, I didn't see a compelling reason to return to any. There was nothing novel to challenge me. I would rather continue onward to countries I haven't yet seen than return to unremarkable ones.

Tallying the number of countries I have been to is not as straightforward as one might assume. It depends on what one considers to be a country and what counts as having been there. By most official numbers, there are 196 sovereign nations on Earth, but the dividing lines are not always drawn so clearly. The United Kingdom, for example, exists politically as a single nation, yet is considered by many to be culturally distinct enough for England, Wales, Northern Ireland, and Scotland to all be considered their own cultures. The sovereign nation of Ireland still holds opposition to the UK, despite being surrounded by it. I made it a point to visit each of these "countries" briefly when I visited to the UK last summer. The UK also holds dominion over 14 British Overseas Territories (BOTs), such as the British Virgin Islands and Bermuda, oceans away. After Morocco, I crossed by ferry back to Spain and stayed the night in the peninsular BOT of Gibraltar. I am happy to include this territory as my 45th visited "country."

Then there are a number of disputed territories whose inhabitants consider them sovereign, but which are nevertheless overlooked by most world powers. Each has claims of ownership imposed by stronger political entities. By some counts, there are 124 countries engaged in active disputes over 105 territories. Taiwan, for example, claims independence from China and is recognized as such by at least 25 other nations. Try mentioning this to anyone in China though, and you might find yourself deported or getting a free tour of a Chinese prison cell.

Last year, I had the opportunity to visit the disputed territory Artsakh, known in English as the Nagorno-Karabakh Republic, while researching my family lineage in Armenia (a nation with a long history of border disputes). While Artsakh is culturally Armenian, it falls just over the Azerbaijani border. Armenians and their descendants are permanently banned from entering the entire country of Azerbaijan. To enter Artsakh through Armenia is considered illegal entry into Azerbaijan. It is grounds for imprisonment or persona non-grata status. To enter Artsakh, I obtained a visa at their embassy in the Armenian capital, Yerevan. Artsakh has its own flag, government, and passport. Yet, because the United Nations does not recognize Artsakh, it is left off almost all official dossiers. Still, I am going to include it in my personal list of visited countries.

Though I was born a citizen of the United States, I sometimes travel on an Armenian passport, which allows me visa-free entry to some former USSR areas that would otherwise be restricted to Americans. It even enables indefinite tourist stays in some places. I was fortunate enough to acquire my Armenian citizenship in 2016 due to my ancestry two generations back. As a little girl, Grandma Goekjian, along with many other religiously persecuted Armenians, fled the Turkish-led genocide 100 years ago to come to Los Angeles. Armenia happens to be one of a handful of countries with an active citizenship-by-descent program for people who can prove to be descended from a citizen of the nation. I had to procure the birth certificates and other documents necessary to show that my grandmother was born in Armenia. A few months later, Armenia welcomed me into the ranks of their citizenry. Countries with similar programs include Bulgaria, Croatia, Ireland, Israel, Italy, Lithuania, Poland, Rwanda, Serbia, Turkey, and Ukraine, though the specifics of each country's program vary.

Some countries, like Russia, have become notoriously stringent about letting Americans in, even as tourists. Intrusive forms must be completed long in advance of any planned trip to secure a visa. I was able to forego all of that because Armenia and Russia are on friendly terms. Likewise, if I ever want to go to Uzbekistan, Mozambique, Iran, or even Brazil, I will be treated with hospitality and visa-free entrance I would not receive traveling on my American passport.

There is also the question of what it means to have been to a place. If one were to count airport layovers or rapid transit through one country to arrive at another (such as my situation of quickly passing from Poland to Belgium through Germany), it would be easy to add numbers to a traveler's list. It's common in Europe to pass through multiple small countries during a single 20-hour train ride. But have you actually "been" there if you've never even stepped off the train? For my purposes, I feel I need to have legally entered the country and spent a day observing the lifestyle of the people. A few months ago, I took an overnight trip from Zagreb, Croatia to Ljubljana, Slovenia and back again to meet friends. That passes the mark for me, though other travelers may use different standards.

Mark Twain's famous saying that "travel is fatal to prejudice, bigotry, and narrow-mindedness" is incomplete. Your firsthand experience of a place can either remove or reinforce stereotypes. How this happens depends on how your preexisting expectations align with actual observation. If you are too rigid in your beliefs, you will only experience new cultures through the lens of confirmation bias. That is what causes a filtered mind to pay attention to only what it is prepared to see or what it can integrate into its working paradigm. However, to throw those generalizations away completely would also be a mistake. They may contain valid information that could save you time, energy, and unnecessary suffering.

Negative cultural biases are sometimes at least partially based in reality. You will find unsavory aspects of any population if you look hard enough. You may choose to ignore these observations and retain a politically neutral outlook. Maybe you think you are avoiding discrimination in a situation you don't fully understand. You wish to maintain certain comfortable illusions about a place you cherish, but you may also pay the price when the reality of the situation confronts you.

When you travel, you exist within a foreign cultural narrative. To live in their world, you will adapt yourself to fit within the limits of their perception. If you move too far from the paradigm of acceptable behavior, the social immune system will make you correct your course. Each mind is only prepared to perceive certain things. If you are going to thrive for any length of time, you must observe what values have influenced the behavior of others around you. As you grow cognizant of their expectations, you will begin to see your own prejudices more clearly.

If you were to venture to Iraq anytime soon, you might feel an unspoken malaise of unease. Although there may be no bombs going off around you, you will still see the effects the possibility of such actions has had on the people. During my three months in Iraq in 2013, I worked at a private educational institution in Erbil in the northern Kurdish region, far from the more violent capital of Baghdad. With traces of civilization dating back to 5,000 B.C. in the citadel, it holds the record as the longest continually habited place on Earth. As I rode from the airport into the city with the school director, I reminded her that this was my first time in the Middle East. It would be important for her to tell me ahead of time if there were any culturally sensitive behaviors I should avoid. Although Kurdish herself, she had lived for many years in the UK, so she understood well how different Iraq could be. She told me there was nothing major to worry about, and she would go over any little things like that in due time.

We pulled into a restaurant and an olive-toned young woman in a hijab took our order. As the director got up from our table, I asked our waiter about life in Erbil. When the director saw me engaged in conversation with this young woman, she grabbed my arm with mouth agape. In a hushed but firm tone, she warned me never to start casual conversations with young Iraqi girls in public. It was at this point she chose to disclose to me that if word were to get back to that girl's home that she had been flirting with a white man, it was likely her brothers and father would beat her. In the worst case, it could result in an honor killing, which is their culturally approved way of justifying the murder of family members for the sake of maintaining the family's honor. It is estimated that at least 1,000 women per year are murdered in this fashion by their families as a result of having sex outside marriage, marrying outside the faith, or being the victim of rape.

In July 2016, honor killings came under greater public scrutiny after the model Qandeel Baloch, the "Kim Kardashian of Pakistan," was strangled to death by her brother. Her crime? Bringing shame on the family by posting social media photos that were too sexy. Honor killings remain legal or carry meaningless punishments in many Islamic parts of the world. And there I was, wondering why the school director had not bothered to mention that to me as a cultural nuance to be aware of beforehand. I learned to tread lightly in Iraqi society after that incident, though I never did find out if the girl from the restaurant suffered any consequences for my ignorance of their instructions for living.

While I faced little hostility as a young American in Iraq, there were countless oddities that betrayed that something was not quite right. The school I taught at was private and expensive to attend. It maintained strict academic standards so that the primary and secondary students would appear impressive on an international level after graduation. The student body was composed partially of local Kurdish children, refugees from Syria and other war-torn neighboring nations, and Europeans who had married locally. Police with fully automatic weapons were stationed on major roads leading up to the high walls of the school. Every morning, the school buses were checked underneath for explosives before entering the gates.

During my short time there, a local political election prompted activists to blow up an ambulance in protest. That is the invisible part of a culture that is so difficult to understand until you experience it yourself. It doesn't show up in the clothes they wear, or the design of their homes, or the things they eat. Iraqis inhabit a world where the destruction of public medical services is an acceptable, even expected, way to express frustration. Beating or murdering one's daughter is considered the responsible way to parent. It's impossible to say what other everyday atrocities I missed in my little window into their world.

It is only through your daily micro-interactions with the people there do you begin to see the unspoken limits to their cultural paradigm. You will begin to realize that the limits you inherited in whatever place you came from are just as arbitrary as theirs. You will need to see beyond them if you are going to truly empathize or if you truly wish to grow. Never in the deepest recesses of my young Californian mindset would I have arrived at such conclusions, no matter what the situation. Somehow, living under the conditions they do, Iraqis develop a completely different schematic for operating in the world. Despite the obvious unsustainability of these values, major groups continue to learn and act in such overwhelmingly anti-human ways.

Sandwiched along the Mediterranean coast between France and Italy sits a micro-nation less than one square mile in size. Within that tiny space are 36,000 residents. Roughly 30% of them are millionaires, the highest concentration in the world, with the highest per capita income globally. The entire country is practically a resort unto itself, with luxury hotels, casinos, restaurants, and high fashion outlets filling every street. This is Monaco.

Extremes on either end, rich and poor, developed and undeveloped, pleasant and unpleasant, give context to the traveler's experience. In many parts of the world, you will find the common people sleeping in shacks beside dirt roads, if not directly in the dirt itself. These realizations can be challenging to the uninitiated, but the mind eventually adjusts to accept this standard of living as baseline. Those who live this way have always had it as their conception of normal.

A fast transition from extreme squalor to a place like Monaco, where thousand-euro-a-night palace suites are the norm, is mentally jarring. The mind needs time to adjust to new conditions. Impoverished inhabitants of many African nations have learned to accept hunger and poor sanitation as part of their culture. The millionaires, who spend their days dressed to the nines, riding in yachts and helicopters instead of walking barefoot across hot African asphalt, have learned to accept theirs too.

It's easy to cast judgment on either of these extremes from the middle, but criticism is idle. It's more important for the traveler to realize the full scope of what is possible, as knowing both extremes exist simultaneously, sometimes even as neighbors sharing a border, promotes genuine empathy. You can remain distant when you are exposed to either side of the spectrum, or you can choose to consciously examine what has led to each side's state. If you look at the way each group has been trained to think and the choices they must make to fulfill their needs, you will see that you might have made the same choices. In the context they were provided, these are the conclusions they have reached. Few members of any culture take the time to step outside of themselves and assess their own behavior. That is what the traveler earns through his or her years of personal expansion. What matters is the willingness to question life's arbitrary starting conditions.

Whether you come from wealth or poverty, or whatever you believe, it is possible to change. Travel is the most rapid way to satisfy that line of inquiry some people will ever know. Travel will not only give you the opportunity to ask uncomfortable questions... it will force you to find meaningful answers. Even in the legal domain, the things you take for granted back home will be proven arbitrary in absurd and inhumane ways. In Singapore, the possession of chewing gum carries a $1,000 fine. This policy has nothing to do with the gum itself, but with people's history of littering it in unsightly and expensive ways. Singapore prides itself on cleanliness and presentation to a degree of social insanity.

While Americans celebrate that gay marriage is finally becoming more accepted, homosexuality is still illegal in 74 countries around the world (including oh-so-modern Singapore). In 13 nations, it is punishable by death through execution or public stoning. Even in many places where it is not illegal, being gay is still forbidden by culture. This prejudice stands in stark contrast to a country like Thailand, where young boys are encouraged to crossdress and cement themselves with the gender identities of Thai girls. They consider themselves neither homosexual men nor biological women. In their minds, they embody a third distinct category, as infamous, hypersexualized ladyboys.

The great paradox of travel is how it can at once seem so old and new. To someone who only travels once or twice a year for leisure, 45 countries may sound impressive. From my perspective, I've been alive just over 28 years. The first 18 were spent in

Southern California, where I rarely ventured even into the nearby states. In the decade since, I've seen 1/5 of the world's territories and only a fraction well enough to feel as though I've resided there. If I look through the eyes of a global citizen, a true "man of the world" who sees the whole planet as his home, I have barely scratched the surface of what is possible. Travel is a rare practice where one can be both a tried-and-true expert and still green. There is too much to witness. One standard human life cannot take it all in.

I've chosen my route because it was what I thought I needed to push my boundaries at specific junctures in my development. After I became comfortable with Latin America, I threw myself into Asia to experience a new level of cultural unfamiliarity. After Asia, it was Western Europe and the Middle East. Aside from Morocco and Ghana, Africa remains largely unexplored for me, but that is something I plan to rectify as I grow bored with the other areas I have adapted to. What comes after that is yet unknown to me. I will figure it out when the time is right.

I would never have guessed, when I began all those years ago, that I would visit all the places I have or survived such strange encounters. I could not have known that I would enjoy some of the places I once could not even locate on a map. It was impossible to envision then how big the planet really was. That is what you learn when you journey for the sake of self-expansion. You say "yes" to things because they challenge you, not because they are necessarily enjoyable. Negative experiences end up being profoundly more valuable than the positive ones, in hindsight.

If you don't travel, the concepts you hold of different places come from a biased media, secondhand from other travelers, or derived from hard statistics that could never capture the experiential essence of a place. When I compare the impression I have of the world now to when I was just a Californian, I wonder how so many people living in modern nations can care so little. I wonder how people spend their whole lives never questioning what lies just a short plane ride away. That is a life I could never fathom for myself: to ignore the nagging curiosity about what else is out there waiting to be known.

The real limits in life are the ones we use to structure our thinking. When someone thinks they have the answer to something, they stop taking in new information about it. The goal of a perpetually evolving person is to cease capping their knowledge in arbitrary places. The Dunning-Kruger Effect explains how people with the least knowledge often have the highest confidence in themselves. It is only when they have crossed a certain threshold that they realize how little they actually know. It's another way of saying that people are often too stupid to realize how stupid they are. Or if you prefer the Tao Te Ching, "those who think they know never learn."

Unfamiliar things are not what frighten people. Fear comes from not knowing one's place in the unfamiliar, which we interpret as an attack on who we are. Ideas that run counter to our identities hurt us. We cannot easily make room in the mind. I could not live the life I do today had I not learned to let go of who I once was. The loss of everything I held onto then, everything I defined myself by, hurt for a time. But then it would never hurt me again. There is a danger of this process happening too fast. One may not be able to handle the pain. The resulting trauma could permanently stop them in their journey. A controlled descent into one's lowest point is the only way for most people to break free of their ruts. You must find your own most direct path from the outskirts of your identity to its core. It is a point you will reach when you have found the mechanism to unravel who you are.

To embrace the unfamiliar is to open oneself up to everything that one can possibly become. It is only a matter of time before your mind will begin to find the tools you can use to get what you need next. Your emotions will adjust to the new demands of your environment and calm your frustration when something doesn't work out the way you expect. Everything you consider familiar in your life was once foreign. You adapted to function in your first home. You will do the same when you expand your home to include the many variations of human culture.

PART 4

Trials & Challenges

Adapting in the Face of Adversity

As you expose yourself to novel circumstances abroad, you are going to change in unseen and uncountable ways. You will become something more than what you were when you started. This happens with simple practicalities – things like where to eat or sleep, or how to make money or maintain relationships when location is no longer a determining factor. But it doesn't end there.

More importantly, it happens in the way you perceive information itself. Your story about the world will change and so will the way you relate to it. Your role within the story will transform into something new and there will be times when it is tempting to rest within a particularly comfortable narrative. To the novice traveler, reading guidebooks and sticking to "Westernized" parts of the world is the best way to stay safe within your zone of familiarity. But to the reckless explorer, taking in the unexpected in every moment is what keeps the excitement alive and their identity growing.

To travel on a regular basis requires dealing with unexpected situations as they arise, as you cannot prepare for every contingency beforehand. You will also lose the opportunity to spontaneously explore new places if you feel you must rigorously study them beforehand. Taking moderate preparations in advance is seldom a bad idea, but you will, in time, learn to trust your innate ability to read a situation and act appropriately within it.

When you were a young child, you learned in the moment which actions caused pain and which satiated your desires. You had parents and countless environmental structures around you that were devoted to your safety – although you had no way of knowing all this at the time. There were safeguards beyond safeguards. Now you must act for the first time with no safety net or assurance. There are no governing bodies to protect you from what you do not know or do not even know that you do not know. You must discover these things with each footstep as you tread into increasingly darker territories. With each discovery, you will grow more capable of taking on the next. You just need to learn the rules of each cultural system as you go.

To thrive in the natural world, you must understand the ecosystem that has evolved around them. You must observe how other successful creatures have adapted to the resources and limitations provided. The survivor quickly learns what actions will help or hurt their situation. Add human beings to any system, and the variables for comfort become immensely more complex. The social domain is built upon the psyches of each participant interacting with one another. Their collective values manifest in everything from the look of the architecture to the laws they enforce. This is how "normal" is born. Every society is a system, and anyone can learn how the system works, manipulate its variables, and find their place within it. Each of these systems perpetuates a pattern of values onto its children that sits at the base of the collective identity as something sacred and unquestionable.

Forgetting old ideas is intrinsically more difficult than taking on new ones. In the transition between old knowledge and new knowledge is a terrifying void of unknowing. In that place, even unconscious certainties – the type of knowledge we take for granted – disappear into unbearable nothingness.

Adventurous people have always longed to explore the potentialities of life on their own terms, but the limits of knowledge and technology made travel a major undertaking. It was difficult, unsafe, and expensive for ships to traverse the oceans or covered wagons to cross continents. They had to know where to go and what might be waiting for them when they arrived. For the first time in history, global residence is now a viable possibility for almost anyone willing to jump through enough bureaucratic hoops. It's more difficult for citizens of some countries than others, but it is possible with enough determination. Despite this modern convenience, most people will never move any significant distance from the place they arbitrarily happened to have been born.

What stops people in the modern age is neither distance nor difficulty. The obstacles are now internal. Innate resistance to change, something that has been with us since the earliest days of exploration, prevents us from taking roads that are now easy to navigate. Physical space is no longer the barrier. It is psychology alone. We need to feel that a way of being is normal and accepted before we can ever begin to consider it for ourselves. Fortunately, for those who wish to travel more comfortably, this is exactly what is now happening with the concept of nomadic living.

The internet allows each of us to collaborate with one another in real time across global borders. The online travel community is evolving rapidly. We are able to reach out to people who share our ideals, no matter where they are from and where they are heading next. Entire sections of the world have taken on specific connotations within the newly formed narrative of the perpetual traveler community. Southeast Asia, for example, is infamous for attracting those seeking warm weather, cheap beer, and pretty little oriental girls who appreciate the charm (and money) of foreign guys. Digital nomad blogs, written by those who work from a laptop as they gallivant from one tropical shore to another, exist to brag about the life-style freedom enjoyed by the authors. They are adorned with picture-perfect snapshots of laptops on beaches, which, if you've ever taken expensive electronics onto the beach, you'll realize is a terrible idea.

Although these voices are the loudest, a global life-style does not have to be this way. It doesn't have to be any specific way at all. This is just another superficial narrative sought by those who were so unhappy with their old lives that they were willing to trade it all in for any story that solved their immediate discontents. Career a mess? Marriage fell apart? Sick of living in your parents' basement? There's a lifestyle narrative for that.

There is no end to the variation. You may choose to relocate every few days. You may set up mini-homes for months at a time. You may become a semi-permanent expatriate in one country for years on end.

There are obvious challenges that travel brings – things like language barriers or safety in unfamiliar places. If you're lucky enough to be a native speaker of English, you'll be glad to know your language has infil-trated nearly every part of the developed world (and a surprising amount of the undeveloped world). Even if the general populace in a place doesn't speak English regularly, there's a good chance they've heard it and can understand basic words and phrases. Or else, they will be able to connect with someone who studied it at university or uses it in a professional capacity.

As economies globalize, more nations encourage or require students to learn at least basic English in school. Adults take it upon themselves to learn the language because they recognize the new professional opportunities it will bring. American television, music, and movies are popular around the world, and local language translations aren't always available. As a former ESL teacher, I can tell you that people learn more practical English by binge-watching episodes of the American sitcom *Friends* than they do by reading educational textbooks.

You'll also find it's not terribly difficult to pick up the basics of English-related languages. Much of the unconscious knowledge you already have of the sounds, vocabulary, and grammar of your native tongue will also apply to Romance languages, like Spanish, Italian, and French. The more of any of these languages you learn, the easier others will also become. To date, the only other language I speak with conversational fluency is Spanish, but I am often surprised at how I can follow a conversation between Brazilians speaking their native Portuguese tongue. Languages with no shared root, however, may challenge some of your most basic assumptions about how communication works, such as the order of words or the different sounds the mouth can make.

It is common that smaller nations with their own official language will still be familiar with whatever the nearest dominant world language is. Although each of the former USSR countries, like Ukraine, Belarus, Georgia, Armenia, and Kazakhstan have local languages, much of the population also speaks Russian. This fact was enough incentive for me to start learning Russian as I traveled through the area, despite having had no intrinsic interest before this. Knowing Spanish will get you around pretty much anywhere in Central or South America, as well as Spain and the surrounding countries in Europe. Arabic covers the Middle East and North Africa. French is spoken throughout former colonies in Africa and parts of Canada. Mandarin is the most spoken language in the world with over a billion native speakers, but most of them are found in China.

Multilinguals are better at moving beyond the arbitrary way they were trained to comprehend reality in words. Learning another language forces one to confront the fact that the way you happened to learn how to think about something is not the only way it can be thought of. Everything is just an interpretation, and there are always other ways to interpret. Learning a country's native language will make you less prone to scams. People won't be able to cheat you. You will not be intimidated by the locals. You can get around better and visit remote areas. You will learn the colloquial-isms and formalities of their culture and gain a deeper understanding. Even if you cannot find a way to com-municate verbally, body language and your tone of voice will do much of the work for you when you learn to use them.

Travel opens the door to changes in some of the most fundamental parts of life. Your concept of rela-tionships with other people will expand – friendly, professional, familial, romantic, or otherwise. All rela-tionships are built upon a shared sense of identity, and non-travelers are unlikely to understand your lifestyle and priorities. That can drive a rift between you (as it did with my former friends and me), or it can have a strengthening effect. Spending an indeterminate time apart from those you care about makes seeing them in three-dimensional space all the more meaningful. Dis-tance is a terrific litmus test for the strength of a bond. Webcam-based relationships aren't fun for anyone, but if you're still excited to see your partner's face each day through a grainy video feed, it's probably a good indicator you actually like this person.

My struggle has been to find the rare gems in any location that I feel I can connect with. Almost every-one remains foremost a product of their culture, so an element from outside it, like me, can confuse or appear outright threatening. Alternatively, some women find the prospect of dating a traveler from another part of the world thrilling. White men are fetishized in some of the same parts of the world where the women are, ironically, fetishized by white men. I don't consider myself a particularly attractive man, but I found that I could hardly walk down a public street in some parts of the Philippines without young girls giggling and shyly turning away. They'd make flattering comparisons with famous American movie stars who no one back home would ever compare me to.

Because I travel so much, women may enter relationships with me carrying no sense of obligation or long-term goals. It took me too many failed relationships to realize that while I had been trying to look past culture and race to build meaningful bonds, most of them only saw me as a passing novelty to spice up the monotony of their lives. We'd get a few months into the relationship, and suddenly they'd forget all about me, ignoring everything we had built up to that point. Or they'd feign interest for the sake of casual dating and fun flirtations but drop the ball and run the moment that real action was needed. Some would begin to get close to me, only to tell me we couldn't proceed any further because they needed to keep their virginity intact if they were to have any chance of finding a husband locally someday.

My most embarrassing relationship non-starter was a slightly older Greek woman I met in an online group specifically created for nomadic people seeking love. We got to a point where we were having video calls for hours every other night before going to sleep, sharing increasingly intimate details about ourselves and our past relationships. She was a therapist who wanted kids as much as I did and shared many of my values. When I booked an apartment in Athens for a month and flew out to meet her, her entire attitude toward me changed. I had to twist her arm into seeing me in person, even though I had only flown out to spend time with her, exactly like we had discussed. I saw her in person for a total of a couple of hours before she suddenly became too busy to see me again or even keep talking to me.

I was never given an explanation as to why there was such a drastic shift from her the moment we shared the same physical space. I can only tell you my interpretation, which is that she thought of me as a novelty to enjoy from afar. The moment our budding relationship became too real and she was forced to deal with the consequences of my existence, she withdrew. These repeated occurrences led me to wonder if it was even possible for me to have a normal relationship with women from any culture. I kept looking, but it seemed hopeless that there was someone out there who shared the values I had earned through the frequent smashing of my boundaries.

Every single person on Earth views the concept of a romantic relationship through the lens they were given growing up in their culture. Their ideas may be different than yours. They may be trying to build an unfamiliar type of structure with you. Unless communication between the two of you is exceedingly good, these invisible differences in your goals may go unnoticed until a breaking point is reached and you are violently forced back onto separate paths. In this way, as in many others, a multicultural lifestyle forces one to mature beyond the arbitrary limits of self-knowledge that others have settled for.

The same can be said for friendships and work relationships. I have made thousands of acquaintances as I've gone around the world. Yet, few showed long-term potential or deep compatibility beyond a surface level need for companionship. I've worked for and with, dozens of companies around the world. I never cease to be baffled by the diversity in professional standards I witness. For the few years I worked as a foreign English language teacher, no two schools were ever alike in their expectations of how I should teach or my role in their hierarchy. Each one acted as though the way they did things was the way that everyone else did and that I should have automatically known all this.

As a freelancer, things weren't much better. A company in India hired me remotely to handle some of their brand strategy and messaging before being impressed enough to invite me out to Delhi so we could upgrade our working relationship. They booked my flight, helped me acquire a five-year Indian business visa, and had an upscale hotel room waiting for me on arrival. I then spent a week observing them struggle to get anything meaningful done before realizing they weren't in a position yet to make full use of my services. They bought me another flight out the next day, now having invested over $2,000 in my travel costs without actually using me for anything. Bafflingly, I stopped hearing from them after that. But at least I got a free trip to India (making country #16 for me).

Relatively late into my travels, I made the decision to stop working for other people. I was tired of doing unfulfilling work on someone else's schedule. I had to trust in my ability to convince strangers to give me money each day to support myself. Self-employment began with small copywriting jobs that were neither emotionally nor financially rewarding for me. By the end of the first week, I realized that there were observable patterns to what people were looking to buy and what kind of person they wanted to work with. I learned how I needed to talk to convince them that I, a stranger on the other side of the world, was somebody they should trust with their money. I changed my approach over time to match what the world showed me it was looking for. I created different offerings at higher prices. I adapted to the environment I had placed myself in, as adaptation was the one thing I was sure I could do.

Since then, I've built a modestly successful online business for myself that I can maintain from anywhere in the world, so long as I can get online from time to time. I've helped many others do the same along the way. People who work online often prefer staying in one place for long periods of time to rapid hopping from place to place. They want to be able to fall into a routine, optimizing productivity while still enjoying the tourism aspects of travel. If you are clever, it's not difficult to keep your living expenses between $500 and $1,500 a month almost anywhere in the world. I eat at home whenever possible. I rent accommodations by the week or the month, instead of the day. I bargain with hotel or guesthouse owners to stay for free if I can improve their online presence or find other ways to help their business.

Checking and sending emails can be done on even the spottiest of connections. Some people need to make frequent audio and video calls on tight schedules to maintain their workflow, or maybe they need to be uploading and downloading large files regularly. Slow internet speeds and unpredictable downtime won't cut it. They must plan more carefully and have back-ups available if their primary connection should fail. In the least developed parts of the world, utilities like electricity and water can shut off daily and at random times, so that one cannot even plan effectively around their interruption. The nature of my field of work grants me the luxury of writing books and producing educational content from a 12" Ultrabook I carry almost everywhere I go, from cross-country bus rides to big city cafes. I can get to work first thing in the morning without getting out of bed if I want. That might sound like hell to you, but it's the kind of freedom I find ideal for maximum productivity.

Most of my first book was written on airplanes and in the back of taxis, whenever I had a spare moment to get more words down. I need only a basic word processor to get the bulk of my work done, but everyone's requirements vary depending on the type of work they do. I even travel with a studio-quality microphone for when I need to do voiceover work on the road, such as the audio narration for this book. Getting on a live video call is crucial to the coaching and consulting work I do, so I must plan these things when I know my internet connection will be reliable. It has to line up with the other party's schedule, which can be difficult when you are several time zones away.

Coordinating projects among teams across many locations makes things even more cumbersome. I now have a policy of only hiring people who can manage their own time and workflow. Dependability is more important than ability when I choose who to work with. I can set up mini-homes for the time when I'm in one place. I interact with people all over the world now and have projects happening in multiple continents. Through video conferencing, phone calls, emails, and shared cloud storage, we manage to get it all done. It makes me wonder why people even bother to do things in person anymore if it's not a fundamental component of their work.

It's not easy to be at home in a new place, but it is vital to develop unconscious comfort quickly. In some situations, you cannot afford to look like an outsider who has no idea what they are doing. Ill-mannered folks are quick to spot the person who looks most out of place in their environment and exploit them for personal gain. Some things about your appearance can't be changed, but you can learn to carry yourself like someone who knows what they are doing.

For better or worse, you will be treated as an anomaly in some places. You may be granted instant celebrity status. People will be eager to get to know you or help you adjust to their country because your existence is so interesting to them. You may well be the first person of your race that the locals have ever seen in person before. It's quite easy to let this go to your head and create an ongoing separation between you and your environment. You might unconsciously accept that you really are better than they are and expect special treatment all the time.

Sometimes, you aren't seen as a person at all – only an opportunity for easy money. You will be targeted for scams and handouts the moment you show up looking out of place, or you will be inundated with the pleas and pitches of shopkeepers and amateur salespeople. They suspect you don't have the same sense of how much things cost, so they will try to convince you to pay high prices for common items. Truthfully, some of my least favorite people in the world are the taxi drivers who amass outside of the bus stations and airport arrival terminals to aggressively solicit to disoriented travelers. The experience is quite dehumanizing and, in my opinion, shows off some of the worst traits of our species. It's the exact opposite of hospitality. It exacerbates the feeling of being unwelcome.

The businessman in me admires the entrepreneurial spirit of their actions. There's a boldness in the cold approach that entrepreneurs from back home could learn from. But my admiration ends there. Almost any engagement confirms their hope that you are open to coercion. The smartest thing to do is to keep your head down and avoid direct confirmation of their presence. They may follow just behind you, asking questions until something triggers a positive response. It's extremely jarring for someone who has just landed in a foreign land and is largely unfamiliar with the language, culture, or geography to be socially bullied like this. Many tourists are pressured into accepting what appears to be free help from these parasitic individuals, followed by borderline threatening demands for money afterward.

Not everyone who offers help is being underhand. People anywhere can be outright kind and generous in their nature and I feel good about giving a little pocket change to someone who saves me time by pointing me in the right direction. But the existence of this scheming class of people makes it difficult to tell the difference between the friendly and the abusive at first glance. They also make it difficult to settle into a new place. My favorite parts of the world are those where this has never been a problem. A few of the forward-thinking societies I have encountered seem to genuinely welcome the benefits that outside money and influence bring into their system. Having to be cautious about engaging with locals discourages me from forging these beneficial connections, or even browsing the local markets and vendors at a leisurely pace. It hurts everyone's opportunities when a few bad apples try to exploit the system in their favor.

Over time, you become less prone to this and other forms of victimization because the way you appear to them changes. Subtle communication evolves as we adapt to a place. That is why the human spam dies off around expats who live a long time in a place. Even if the scammers don't consciously understand what it is, something tells them they won't make viable targets for their scheme anymore. Predators always seek the easiest prey.

What I have earned from the trials I have put myself through is a confidence in my ability to adapt to almost any social context. I have gained this because I've seen enough of what human beings are capable of. I've seen the dark and the light and I haven't turned away from any of it. I now trust myself to observe and learn in any cultural environment, just like in those early days, when I wandered alone into the wilderness of Costa Rica. I learned quickly from my minor mistakes, so they never became major injuries. The same mentality applies whenever I cross into an unknown, potentially unstable country.

It is easy to let these personal advancements go to one's head. You begin to feel superior to normal people, even invincible in your own way. This accumulated pride is not necessarily false, but it is dangerous. You are only paying attention to half the internal spectrum of experience. Opposite the light and warmth of your accomplishments is the darkness of your defeats. If you do not yet know this darkness, you have either been exceptionally lucky or played the game safely so far. Your crushing defeat is still out there, waiting for you to stumble. In that blackest night, you will uncover a new level of personal victory.

PART 5

Approach the Insurmountable

Arriving at the Dark Night of the Soul

The most terrifying experience in the world is not to know who you are, where you're going, or what you're supposed to be doing. To travel without inhibition is to consciously embrace that fear. It is to accept that you do not always know what to do because you do not even know the limits of what is possible. Until you have spent time exploring these limits, you cannot earn confidence in the validity of your life choices.

Many people are uncomfortable traveling on their own, but it is the best way to see things in a new light, unfettered and untainted by the perceptions of others around you. You will see the world without filters, making the influence all the more meaningful. But that influence can also be destructive. There will always be something your mind is not ready to accept as real. It is something that lies outside the limits of your conception – something so awful by your standards of evaluation that it is antithetical to your existence.

You will want to run from it because to let it take hold of you is to experience death. If you do not run, it will break you. To move willingly toward it is to enter the lowest possible point in your life: the dark night of the soul. It is your personal hell and the thing you have spent your entire life avoiding. It may make you nervous even thinking about it. You may now be mounting protestations to keep your consciousness safe from its intrusion. Sooner or later, one must reconcile the fact that there are parts of themselves that remain obscured by darkness and shadow. Any time we have been hurt or believe we have been wronged, we push those instances away from our working awareness. We bury the negative aspects of our personality, relegating these things to where they remain invisible to everyone but ourselves.

We are all burdened by the memories of past actions of which our present selves disapprove. This is where guilt originates – in the knowledge and judgment of self. These elements are never removed. They lurk deep inside our psyche and come out when the conscious mind lapses in the attention it dedicates to homeostasis. The ordinary world starts to shatter. I used to sometimes wake, drowning in negative thoughts about past events, ex-girlfriends, and people whom I felt had wronged me in a million different ways. I was obsessed with myself and people's fair treatment of me. I strove to be both honest and just with the people I included in my life, yet I rarely saw the same investment reciprocated back.

In all my travels, the world still did not make sense to me. It was a system deeply broken in uncountable ways. For me, travel was as much about learning the workings of the world that man has built for himself as it was about learning what I was capable of as an individual. I now realize the two sides are intimately connected, engaged in an unbreakable dance with each other. We build the world, and the world builds us.

No one's first response to pain is to go deeper into it. No one willingly plunges further into the fire. Only a deep inquirer will see the powerful benefit that pain brings when it is managed correctly. The fire burns differently for everyone, and each of us must take it upon ourselves to discover what resides in our dark places. We must address the inferno building inside before it becomes too much to bear. People who never embrace their own pain will not take the actions that are required to solve it, even when those actions are simple. This is the final prison. It is only after they have come through the other side of hell that they are free to live as themselves in the world as it is.

The breaking point comes upon each person in its own time and in its own way. Sometimes, it's the slow burn of an unfulfilling life that eats away at a person's comfort for decades, and the one who is suffering maintains appearances as much as they can. Internally, they wither away until reality rapidly resolves itself in the form of a lifestyle crisis or existential dilemma. You are most susceptible to erratic change when you are deepest in despair.

Many non-travelers view travel as a vehicle for crisis resolution. They don't expect it to bring them deeper into the crisis. They pull an 'Eat Pray Love' and embark on a soul-searching voyage abroad. Like Elizabeth Gilbert, I too have lived in Ubud on the island of Bali for months at a time on two occasions. It's a pleasant enough place, but hardly worthy of the spiritual pilgrimage she describes. By refusing to confront the real pain and the problem from which it stems, they only perpetuate their suffering under more attractive settings. The wheel keeps turning, and the cycle begins anew. A lifestyle reboot means having enough self-awareness to want something fundamentally different than what you already have. Where people fail is that they lack the endurance to seek out the root causes of why they suffer. They cease the search when things get difficult, leaving them susceptible to easy answers in whatever form they appear.

Not everyone who begins the journey is looking for truth. They are looking to ease the discomfort of inquiry. This is the great delusion that all seekers must guard themselves against. The temptation to quit early is strongest when the most progress is being made. In those moments, you must choose to keep going – or risk reverting to the state in which you started. This process only happens through total vulnerability. In vulnerability, you grow because you must. You discover just how far you can push yourself. If you don't respond to the outside forces that weaken you, they will break you. Your character strengthens, and you develop a thicker skin for the experiences that would normally destroy you. You learn to relish instability because that is where all progress happens.

Stability means that nothing ever changes, which is only a good thing if you are already living the life of your dreams. In both chemistry and personal development, instability creates the possibility for new events. Stability is only the rational goal of a person who knows who they are and what will make them sustainably happy. People fear the unknown because they cannot prepare for what might go wrong. In a known environment, it's easy to arrange the factors of your life toward the attainment of your goals, even if you must improvise along the way. When the things you take for granted are pulled away, you lose the faith that everything will work out in your favor.

You also cannot assume that everything will go wrong all at once. Life tends to happen within a predictable range of good and bad occurrences that must be adjusted to in real time. You must trust that your mind can take in the information it needs as it experiences new things. It uses this information to create new instructions for living as needed. "What if" scenarios can be a form of mental poison. There is rarely a single realistic event with the power to utterly ruin one's life unless one throws complete caution to the wind. If unanticipated variables change – perhaps your trip is extended, a flight is missed, or a bag is misplaced – we adjust to them in the moment to stay on the path of comfort.

Travel for self-expansion requires one to let go of these old standards of predictability. You cannot foresee everything. There is no way to pack your suitcase adequately for this kind of trip, and no concierge to manage all the missteps for you. You must take it upon yourself to become the type of person who oversees the governing elements of your own in life in every moment. A successful person knows themselves intimately, to a degree far beyond the endurance of ordinary humans. The boundaries of familiarity stretch as far as they can. So long as one can recover from injury, they can gain from the intentional exposure to pain. Curiosity will drive them with uncertain enthusiasm forward. This is the true start to the self-directed path.

Early in my travels, I became a teacher because something in me was deeply curious about how our world passed on old values to new generations. Working in education gave me a unique insight into the parts of culture normally hidden from outsiders and casual tourists. It also gave me a deep resentment for those who maintain their culture at the cost of corrupting young minds. I was consumed by the fire of seeing children made into vessels for arbitrary cultural values on a massive scale. Interacting with humans at every stage of development showed me that what most countries call education is a form of cultural narcissism. Whatever is important to the prevailing authorities must also be made important to up-and-coming citizens. Because the old crop of humans believe in something, so too must the new crop. In witnessing this generational transfer of values, I knew the true enemy of progress.

To burn in hell is to see the complete dismantling of your core values within and around you. Because my new environments allowed me to explore myself, I became aware of how much I cared about nurturing and protecting potential. I developed a deep affinity for children and animals because they were unaffected by the corrupting influence of culture. But everything casts a shadow. By choosing to care, I opened the possibility of losing what I cared for. My most life-affirming experiences were followed by my most destructive – experiences that would push me past a psychological breaking point I didn't know I had.

I see now it was necessary for me to survive a deep emotional pain unique to my experience of reality. From this, I learned that anything that holds power over us does so for important reasons. Enslavement, in fact, can teach us more about ourselves than freedom.

More than anything, travel has shown me the full breadth of what humans are capable of. I learned that the worst of humanity is not our ability to commit momentary acts of violence or personal oppression; it is how we rear children to live as receptacles for our own outdated ideologies and traditions. The dignity of humanity lies in our ability to think for ourselves. The unconscious acceptance that culture must flow to new generations actively suppresses this dignity.

By the time I booked my first trip to Asia to work as an English teacher in China, I had already seen many new types of extremes in the world. China blew them all out of the water. There, I discovered that a place existed where each day human beings were packed shoulder-to-shoulder in the street, and where homogeneity ruled. There was so much to see, but so little variety. It felt both dystopian and surreal to become a functioning part of the social machine that existed to remove each individual's individuality.

Through my daily interactions, I learned that the Chinese did not appreciate questions about the way things were in their lives. They had no reason to conceive of alternatives. Cultural awareness of life outside the empire was practically non-existent. The Chinese government was masterfully efficient at controlling the flow of information from within and outside its walls. As a result, the average person would only think things their political rulers condoned.

The control of information exerted by the Chinese government is the most impressive in the world. Only 34 foreign movies are allowed into the country every year, a number that was even lower until recently. Any form of media that portrays China in a negative light is instantly banned. Limited acceptance has led to certain major blockbusters pandering to China to get on the limited list of approved releases and earn revenue from the lucrative Chinese market.

The internet, the greatest enabler of inquiry, communication, and collaboration in human history, is also heavily censored in China. Thousands of websites, including such giants as Facebook, Google, and YouTube, are stuck behind the "great firewall of China." Dedicated dissidents can still access social media and unregulated search engines if they are willing to connect through a virtual private network (VPN) that masks their computer's IP address in another country – but to do so is illegal.

The official explanation for China's Orwellian policies over the flow of information is that they are in place to protect the Chinese economy from outside competition, or because Chinese citizens would run the risk of stumbling onto pornography and other harmful material if there were no strict limits on accessibility. Such is the story everyone I met in China was raised to believe. Few ever questioned it. As someone who values learning and inquiry so deeply, it was unsettling to live among such unconsciously imprisoned people.

Although China is ostensibly a non-religious nation, their government has become the primary object of deification throughout the culture. During Chairman Mao Zedong's "Cultural Revolution" in the 1960s and 70s, billions of copies of his infamous *Little Red Book* were printed and distributed, with the goal that 99% of the entire Chinese population would read, own, and carry a copy with them at all times. Though Mao's reign is over, my experiences there showed me they still maintain a similar level of reverence for their masters even now. This was another significant blow to my ideals of independence and self-mastery.

In the 1990s, a spiritual movement based on qigong and meditation called Falun Gong spread rapidly among the Chinese people. The government implemented a plan to eradicate Falun Gong because they saw its success as a threat to their authority. Propaganda emerged labeling practitioners as insane and traitorous to the nation. Since the Chinese government keeps no public records of its genocidal behavior, it can only be estimated how many followers of the practice they have arrested and executed. Evidence even exists that they farmed their victim's organs so they could be transplanted into the more highly valued citizens of the Chinese empire.

The Falun Gong campaign came to a head in 2001, when five people committed suicide by fire under the public's gaze in Tiananmen Square. The government was quick to concoct a story that the demonstrators were dangerous people driven to madness by their practice of Falun Gong. No independent investigation into the incident was allowed, despite the fact that the movement teaches against violence of any type. I can obviously never confirm these stories and what they imply about the Chinese ruling class, but what I observed in my time there did little to paint a more favorable picture.

While in the coastal city of Dalian – one of the wealthiest parts of the country – a train derailment caused by poor track maintenance killed dozens of passengers. I learned from the mother of a family I was tutoring for, who had connections in the local government, that any records which showed the deceased and their luggage had ever been aboard were eliminated before the local media could file their reports. As far as the rest of China was concerned, no one had died in the accident. Anything that could be used as evidence of government neglect was similarly wiped from public eyes before it became known.

Between working in government schools and privately in the home of this wealthy family, I was shown an informative and uneasy view of real life in China. Chinese culture demands that all children remain unquestioningly submissive to their parents until adulthood. Adults then spend the rest of their lives taking care of their parents until they pass away, and the cycle continues with their own children. The irony of this hyper-authoritarian parenting approach is that children spend up to 16 hours a day away from home in school, being raised more by their understaffed institutions and dogmatic curriculum than their parents. Such is the genesis of their group thinking and group identification.

Six months living in these comfortably uncomfortable conditions changed something deep within me. I started to fall apart from the inside. I became unconsciously suicidal, a terrifying state colored not by an active desire to end one's life or experience pain. It was as if my body's automatic will to survive withdrew at the most arbitrary of times. Simple pleasures and self-maintenance lost all meaning. There was no difference for me anymore between life and death, except that life required more effort.

I've always been the kind of person who reveled in challenges. I run toward discomfort because it is always a chance to improve myself. I trust that I am capable enough to turn whatever doesn't kill me into an opportunity for self-improvement. But China showed me a completely alien kind of suffering. There was nothing to push against there – no resistance to plow through. Momentum was draining from my identity, and I had no resources to work with. There was no-where to turn and no externalities upon which to fo-cus my discontent. So, I broke.

This break was only possible because of the specific internal circumstances I had created for myself during my years in Latin America. Unknowingly, I had set myself up for the deepest kind of devastation a person can withstand. Because I had discovered my authentic values, I opened the door to the destruction of those values. I was just beginning to be confident in who I was. I knew what I cared about and what I was willing to invest myself into. I had unknowingly set the stage for my greatest downfall in the form of despair that proved so great it would have been impossible to feel under the guise of my old life.

China showed me that everything has an anti. The stronger the proclamation, the greater its opposite. A person of principle who pursues great action cannot be neutral. By putting your foot down, you open your-self up to attack. In learning how much I cared about social harmony and human expression, I also learned that the suppression of these things had the power to break me. I could not have one without the other or go back to a state of neither knowing nor caring. For the first time, I knew I did not want to live in a world where it was possible for the things I witnessed to ex-ist in the ways they did.

The trials of my path allowed me to uncover what lies at the core of my identity. My fundamental self was nothing more than a force to nurture the potential of the world in its many vulnerable forms. I stripped away the non-essential elements of my experience of myself to find only something elemental that wanted to protect innocence and dismantle inhumanity. I didn't seem like a person anymore. Like anyone else, I still had the memories, preferences, flaws, and attachments that define a person. But under that surface layer was a principle more important to my perception of self and my operation in the world. It was an unwavering commitment to a particular brand of ideals. I would never be satisfied with a life shaped by the expectations of others. Loneliness and isolation from my species weighed me down. But it was my path.

The path was no longer about overcoming the past. It was about preparing for the existential challenges of the future. I had inadvertently defined my battles already by aligning myself with the values I held. The same values would define everything about my life and actions. I, as a person, would work to become the human form of these values – a form for which the rest of world already had a label and a story.

It would take me many months away from China to recover from the trauma it instilled in me, but I would eventually realign myself with my goals. That new perspective on the potential darkness of human behavior is now invaluable to my assessment of self and environment. I understand with certainty what it means to live without the things I hold dearest and to stick to my principles in a world that seems apathetic or opposed to them.

That pain is my constant companion and a reminder of why I strive. It gives me focus and protects me from endless superficial distractions. I'm uncertain if it is possible for a person to understand who they are and what they are looking for without surviving a total deconstruction of self such as this. I only know it was necessary for me, as the person I was, to walk to the brink of my personal abyss and remain there long enough to find peace with it. I know what it would take to destroy me. Everything casts a shadow, and everyone must sooner or later encounter theirs.

People fear this much boundless responsibility because they are used to relying on the past to shape their future actions. They've never had the opportunity or the obligation to look at their own lives in the context of the opposite. They don't know what it means to ask themselves what they want – which is another way of asking what conditions will bring them the most happiness or unhappiness. They aren't familiar with their fundamental limits because they have never approached them. The intimate knowledge of the limits of my existence was the lasting gift that the organized evils of China gave me.

Every dark night of the soul is a rare opportunity for a deeper level of self-reflection, but only if the darkness is embraced. Sometimes things need to get worse before they can get better. What prevents you from reaching your negative depths is your own fear of what you will learn about yourself. A person who exists as a collection of memories and social expectations cannot ever experience what it means to encounter the dark forces working against them. Only a principle is privy to that dreadful luxury.

PART 6

Victory and Rebirth

Discovering New Ways to Exist

The way you have learned to live as the person you are is not the only way things could have gone. Reared under different philosophies, with a different name and new values, you would have become a different expression of the potential within you. When you've reached the limits of what your starting conditions can offer you, you owe it to yourself to break free as you move into the world of internal possibilities. The process begins with a sense of loss, but it doesn't end there. With destruction comes the seeds of creation, but only if you have the endurance to see the cycle through to the other side. When you have embraced the loss of everything you once were, you will learn to see every situation from multiple angles. You will understand that there are infinite other ways to solve the same problems and infinite other problems with which to concern yourself.

Making peace with what you thought would destroy you makes you psychologically invulnerable because you free yourself from the dead past of tradition. The space it occupied is now empty. What you fill it with will determine the course of your life from that day forward. Then you can rebuild your life in a new image, untethered to the chains of the past. You can arrange the variables of your life to be specifically and personally appealing. To do this, you must understand who you are and how you will react under different conditions. You must rediscover yourself.

As children, we had unlimited ideas about what we would do with our lives. By the age of 25, most of us will have resigned ourselves to repetition and routine. It grows easier with each passing day to perpetuate the familiar. Our tastes grow ever more confined with time. We have forgotten discovery as an active state.

Peak discovery is intimidating to ordinary people because they define themselves by their limits. They have forgotten how to look beyond what they know. There was a time when you didn't think about how foolish you might feel if you were not immediately good at something. Trying new things was once endlessly exciting for each of us. Adults lose this freedom with age because they rigidify their concept of self. To display any weakness at all is to murder the conception of self – a fate worse than actual death.

Left unchecked, specialization closes the mind to new experiences. Our specializations become our jobs, our hobbies, and how we describe who we are to the world. We get so used to labeling ourselves by a certain set of terms that we disregard any others. Who you are becomes nothing more than an unconscious script you carry with you. Cultural dogma tells us that identity expansion ends in early adulthood. New skills and abilities are acquired when we are young or not at all. Common knowledge convinces us that who we are when we finish schooling is who we are destined to be forever. In my observation, this bleak outlook is one of the most common traits around the world.

Young children get away with errors that adults do not because no one expects someone with such limited life experience to perform well at anything. As adults, we learn to be ashamed when we hit a wrong note on the piano or make an inaccurate remark on an esoteric subject. There's far less forgiveness for the grown man or woman who ought to know better. Grown-ups are not given the leniency they need to attempt something they cannot accomplish.

The paradox of learning in adulthood is that we have greater abilities, resources, and experience than ever before, but we cannot take in new information as readily as we once did. We go narrower and deeper into knowledge but are easily overwhelmed by anything outside our familiarity. Because children have no strong familiarity, they forego this resistance. That is their unique advantage over us. Their natural enthusiasm makes all the difference. They don't fear the discomfort of pushing personal boundaries. When people stop learning, they exist only to perpetuate the way they have been trained to see until now. Their actions preserve the world by applying the standards of those who came before them. They learn the rules of life and spend every moment being used by those rules – a slave to their own knowledge. Overcoming the belief that learning is difficult can be a bigger challenge than learning itself, but it is vital to continued growth.

It is often complete newcomers to a subject who most readily adopt the principles of adeptness. Prior experience creates predisposition. We inherit biases from those who already know what they are doing. Experts are limited to old information because the mind is already occupied. They cannot entertain multiple ideas within the same category without accepting one as absolutely true. Worldviews grow narrower with time. Regardless of the power of the intellect, emotions are not fluid enough to make perpetual change possible. Only blank slates don't have to fight against the inertia of experience. If you've been working the same job, living in the same town, running with the same social circle, and dealing with the same problems, you will have forgotten the thrill of childlike discovery.

Everything in life is constantly changing – in a state of advancement or decline. Without the impulse to explore, we lose ourselves to patterns of convenience. People cannot see what will move them toward bigger and more attractive goals – if they have any explicit goals at all. They have no trouble filling their days with trivial pursuits but cannot plan their life out on a larger scale. By intentionally exposing yourself to new influences, you cannot help but make meaningful progress. You will mature faster through alternatives to what you already believe.

Throughout my childhood, I struggled to adapt to the ways others expected me to act. I felt I lacked what others had naturally – an automatic understanding of what I was supposed to do next. I had to begin analyzing human behavior by always looking for subtle clues in speech and body language to reveal a person's unconscious expectations. It started my obsession to understand the many ways that people could live with each other on our planet. Eventually, I learned that I could beat them at their own game, mastering social adaptation and targeted communication.

Those born with disadvantage respect the details that others take for granted and so bring greater perspective. Such is the unique power of the human race. We can expand our psychological selves through knowledge and practice. Through conscious death, the social, emotional, and mental obstacles to expansion are removed. Then comes rebirth. When you make it a point to learn as many of the rules of life as possible, you stop being a slave to them. They start to work for you because you can pick and choose how to apply or ignore them. You gain a freedom of choice beyond that of ordinary men and women. You are liberated enough to shape the world around you in the way you want it, instead of it shaping you for its own needs. That is the power that lies on the other side of death and rebirth. You become a creator.

It's often said people die shortly after retiring. When they retire from the tasks they've spent their life performing, they lose their place in the narrative of life. Maybe they take a year or two to loaf on the beach or play golf at their leisure. But with nothing left to make demands on their time, their assumed identities start to crumble. They cannot figure out what to do with the freedom life affords them. They've never had to choose what to do without other obligations.

Lifestyle design is about taking the control you have and forging a path tailored to your satisfaction. To be a conscious designer of your environment, you must know what will enable you to thrive. You must know the fundamental limits of who you are. These are the limits we test time and again through inquiry into ourselves and exploration outward into the unknown. When you survive your worst, you gain a perspective that very few others have ever achieved. You have a freedom that is rarely ever found.

Ordinary people don't live this way. They live their lives chasing whatever reaffirms their established selves. Their pursuit of stability leads to complacency, which leads to degradation and death. The same year is lived over and over throughout a person's lifespan. The pattern must be interrupted in a big way for lasting change to happen. Each of us has parts of ourselves that we once learned were unacceptable. Boys are encouraged toward certain activities, while girls are given their own set of rules. Unconventional approaches to intimacy are shunned the world over. We create labels to categorize the things we don't understand as sinful, criminal, or perverse.

Life as an outsider gives you a license to be different. Not only do you not need to worry about upsetting the same rules you acquired back home, but foreigners are not held to the same standards of behavior as the locals. This fish-out-of-water status gives you the opportunity to rediscover who you are. Everything you learned to be ashamed of can be brought to the forefront of your life again. Recall what you cared about before anyone ever told you what to care about. These same qualities still exist within you. They will come up when you have removed the cultural obstacles that have taken their place. Your natural programming will take over if you only get out of your own way long enough to allow it.

That's a very intimidating thought to some people – the idea that there is another you within you, buried underneath the you that you have learned to be. The true self, the higher self, the authentic self... whatever label you want to apply makes no difference. To label this is to still see it as something other than what you actually are. It puts it "out there" in the world, away from you. It keeps you stuck in a cycle of misery. The more you conceptualize it, the further away from it you will end up. How do you arrive at something that gets further from you the more you pursue it?

Because I was broken, I had nowhere else to run but where I already was. When I learned to observe my existence as it was presently happening, without the story about where I came from, where I was going, and what it all meant, I could begin to rebuild my life atop a solid foundation. It gets more difficult with age. There are more falsehoods to be forgotten and a tighter hold over one's conception of self. Older people have more to lose than younger ones, but this does not mean it is impossible. There are real stories of people in their 40s, 50s, and 60s finally coming to meet themselves after a lifetime of searching. They have been fortunate enough to have events conspire around them to bring them to a state where they were ready for the truth. Not everyone receives that blessing in the course of their lives, or they are too blind to see it by the time it arrives.

Ask yourself what has prompted you to begin exploring this path. What has brought you to the point you are right now? Then ask why you have declined to continue just yet. It is either that you don't understand how to or more likely that you've decided to stay in the transitional state a while longer. You worry about what will happen if you commit yourself to rebirth. Let go of the idea that depth needs to wait until its appropriate time. There is no need to prolong your illusions about yourself any longer.

You can commit to learning more about your capabilities with each passing day. You can follow your known passions to their logical extremes. The compounding effects on your personal and professional life will be staggering. You might soon no longer recognize the place you came from. That rapid growth will threaten and confuse others and even yourself if you allow it. It is just you feeling free enough to act like more of yourself in the world around you.

One gains confidence in one's actions through witnessing their success. Confidence, in turn, leads to greater action. Whatever is brewing inside you must turn into real action. This is how new ways to live are discovered – through one unfamiliar act at a time. The spirit of adventure will guide you into these unfamiliar territories. When you are already out of your comfort zone, you have more freedom to try things you normally wouldn't. It will be only your own learned limits that keep you trapped in specific kinds of behavior – whether favorable or unfavorable. Maybe you will find your old hobbies are no longer as satisfying without the environment of home to support them. You will believe that you are losing a little part of yourself when old concerns aren't as important as they once were. Idle curiosity will return, impelling you to branch out.

Life under new conditions enabled me to develop a deep appreciation for science, the arts, and philosophy. I learned to bond with nature. I started to care about animal welfare, education, entrepreneurship, child development, and even writing. These values didn't come from nowhere, and they weren't implanted by the societies around me. They stemmed from an innate facility that found new grounds for expression. I'm still learning, and it is still exciting for me to not be able to predict how different I will be a year from now. I can only see so far around the curving road ahead of me.

People stagnate in life because they do not explore their own behavior in novel ways. Familiar conditions do not allow for it. The unfolding of a person has to start as the response to new stimuli replacing old stimuli. Each person must take the initiative to seek new stimuli in their own time and in their own way. You must have the courage to follow your curiosity wherever it may lead you.

Just as every culture has its weaknesses, there are also uniquely appealing highlights for each. They are all bound by their own rules, and sometimes some of those rules make sense. You are no longer obligated to dedicate yourself to just one way of living or one set of rules to follow. Each system has something it can teach you. The artist seeks to add as many colors as possible to his palette so they will have more options for creative expression. They learn the rules so that they may break them at strategic intervals. Artists re-shape the world in their own image, adding little touches of themselves everywhere they go.

People fear what they cannot categorize, which is another way of saying what they don't understand. You will feel lost for a time without a solid category to belong to. Don't let that fool you into choosing a prem-ature identity. There is no single way to be a traveler, an artist, a scholar, a superhero, or a philosopher. You accept other people's definitions when you are too weak to make your own.

Any time you try something new, you must first learn the parameters of the system you are now part of. You cannot start with the same giant conclusions you see more practiced people display. Change is so intimidating that most people never even get started, and their goals remain forever unrealized. You are scared to change yourself to fit into a system you don't understand. That is why you must be willing to pick apart any new knowledge you encounter. Break it down to its axioms so you can use its governing prin-ciples for your mastery of it.

By default, we define ourselves by the problems that consume our time. These are our attachments.

Without attachments, our identities would be indistinguishable and formless. Without problems imposed into our lives, we create them ourselves. Something must always hold a place of importance in the mind. If our survival is not in jeopardy, we project problems onto something trivial. Total stress remains the same. Things can never be at peace for long. Boredom is unsustainable.

Freedom is choosing for yourself what problems you want to place within your sphere of attachment to solve. You alone are the arbiter of what deserves space in your life, or what is worth facing stress over. If you must have problems, make them problems worth having. Choose your attachments wisely. Figure out for yourself what is worth fighting and dying for – a principle bigger than yourself.

When you see what that thing is, you will be on your way to knowing the principle of you. It is both the pushback against pain and the drive toward accomplishment that leads to change. It is a state of being that ordinary people are terrified to discover because they resist the depths they must trek to arrive there. It is what will show you the new skills and abilities you need to do what you now know must be done. This realization is where your life truly begins.

PART 7

A New Home

Finding Your Place on Earth

Freedom is having total control over the determinants of your life. Different parts of the world restrict the local population's ability to choose their own actions. Limits to action happen through laws and social pressure to always fall within certain limits of acceptable behavior. The only complete escape from cultural restrictions is to abandon civilization entirely. When a person grows secure in their knowledge of themselves, they naturally migrate to where they will be free to live authentically. They want to be part of a culture that celebrates their value – not one that tries to change them. They want to do the type of work they find most rewarding. They seek their place in a crowded landscape.

Today, I look at myself as a man without a culture or a home. Although I still tell people I am from the United States, I do not maintain any pride, loyalty, or identification for my roots there. California is just where I came from – an arbitrary place I happened to have been born and raised for a time. It is no more important to my present self than any of the many places I have been since.

Home can be wherever you're most comfortable – where you can be who you really are. Identifying that place has been part of my quest since I began so many years ago. Peering beyond the imaginary borders that divide our species lets you choose the best that each place offers. A man or woman of the world has the opportunity to bend the rules of each culture toward their personal values. The more you travel, the more options you have to choose from.

"Flag theory" is the idea that the greatest security in life comes from diversifying one's lifestyle, income, assets, and national alignment across different parts of the world where the best conditions for each can be found. It protects you from loss in case of a major destabilizing event and allows you to avoid the weaknesses of any given place, while also taking full advantage of the strengths. It's a powerful expression of a global identity in the modern world.

A person who takes full advantage of flag theory might hold passports in two or three countries across different continents, be a legal resident somewhere else, bank in another jurisdiction, register their remote business elsewhere, and keep their property or other assets somewhere unrelated. On top of all this, they might spend most of their personal time as a tourist in a place they have no other ties to. Because they are comfortable looking beyond national boundaries, they can profit from the unique benefits afforded by each place. The lifestyle variations this opens are endless.

For a global citizen without allegiance to any specific place, passports seem like glorified permission slips from the world's ruling political classes. Although they ostensibly grant greater freedom of movement, they are also effective tools for limiting the actions of the people. Historically, they have been taken away from citizens who did not pay their taxes or showed other unfavorable behavior toward their kings and leaders. In 2016, the United States passed a bill enabling the passport revocation of any citizen who owes more than $50,000 in back taxes – a liability further compounded by the fact that Americans are taxed no matter where they live or from where they derive their income.

Banking in another country seems like it should be a straightforward task. Just walk into a branch with your money and your ID and ask to open an account. Unfortunately, most countries that are stable enough to make storing money a desirable option also make it difficult-to-impossible for non-residents to keep their money there. There are exceptions, but due to the FATCA (Foreign Account Tax Compliance Act) regulations of the US, banks around the world are pressured into reporting the details of any US citizen's account activities back home. This negates many of the advantages of diversifying your funds and has made many banks and nations reluctant to work with Americans at all.

The best place to hold a passport depends on where you plan to travel with it, as well as the amount of effort you are willing to put into obtaining it through legal channels. For someone who often travels in Europe, it's a good idea to get a passport with visa-free access to the Schengen area. Most developed nations outside of the EU will get an automatic 90-day allowance out of every 180 days, but citizens of Third World nations can expect to have to acquire a visa in their home country beforehand. Unfortunately, becoming naturalized as a citizen in most places takes five to ten years of consistent residence and other requirements like running a business with a certain amount of taxable income. There are alternatives, like the citizenship-by-descent program I was able to take advantage of in Armenia or various citizenship-by-investment options for people who have more money than time. The Caribbean island nation of Dominica will essentially "sell" you a passport for a $100,000 non-refundable fee, or $175,000 invested in approved Real Estate. If that sounds expensive, the cost of some other countries' programs ranges into the millions.

It would be nice to live in a world politically evolved enough to allow complete freedom of travel, commerce, and residence. In 1954, political activist

Garry Davis held similar ideals. He founded the non-profit organization the World Service Authority (WSA) to print and distribute what he called the World Passport – a travel document not linked to citizenship in any country and available to anyone who could meet basic identification requirements.

The World Passport is a noble gesture – but an impotent one for now. Only six countries have officially accepted it (Burkina Faso, Ecuador, Mauritania, Tanzania, Togo, and Zambia). Despite its history of more than 60 years, most of the world still considers it an illegitimate fantasy document, useful only for stateless people and crisis refugees with no other option for travel. Although there are anecdotal accounts of travelers getting into more than 180 countries with a World Passport, traveling on it carries a significant risk of being detained or arrested. But that doesn't mean a non-governmental form of citizenship couldn't one day become valid in our rapidly changing world.

Or consider the case of Liberland, the world's youngest prospective micro-nation. Liberland was established in April of 2015 in a small area of no man's land between Croatia and Serbia. President Vít Jedlička, a politician from the Czech Republic, set out to create a country based on open borders, free markets, and cultural inclusivity. Their motto is "Live and Let Live," and they welcome people from all backgrounds, barring doctrines of extremism. Although

Liberland has not yet received much official recognition by the existing world powers, more than 400,000 people have applied for citizenship. Whether it ever takes off as the mecca of progress and prosperity its founders intend, even Liberland's infancy is a sign of evolving ideals about how to structure a society.

In the state of Tamil Nadu, southern India is the town of Auroville, which shares many of the qualities of a modern micro-nation. Established in 1968, Auroville, or the City of Dawn, is backed by the Indian government and protected by UNESCO. It has grown from 400 to around 2,400 residents and is home to expatriates from 49 nations. This town is meant to serve as a model for what human civilization can become if we look beyond the arbitrary distinctions of our societies. Although intended to usher in a spiritual transition to the future, Auroville has reportedly failed to live up to its utopian ideals. Aside from its stagnated popularity, it appears subject to many of the same problems its founders sought to escape. Crime, corruption, and even murder are still present. Although it purports itself to be a "moneyless" society, it still receives ample funding from outside, and residents use funds internally for a crude form of exchange. Additionally, the bureaucratic inefficiencies the founders sought to escape continue to weigh down daily operations. Being based on the teachings of an Indian guru, Sri Aurobindo, it has more of the qualities of a spiritual commune than a global city.

Even the oceans and outer space are not off limits for the modern settler. The Seasteading Institute aspires to create the world's first sovereign floating cities in international waters. Bringing the concept a step further, a private organization calling itself Asgardia desires to launch a satellite into orbit to establish the first nation-state in space. In the digital realm, Bitnation is attempting to build an alternative to contractual state-run services by using cryptography and blockchain technology. Even Estonia is now offering digital e-residency for people who have never set foot in the country (with over 13,000 successful sign-ups in its first 18 months of implementation) and is establishing "data embassies" of government backups on foreign soil. Such initiatives challenge our most basic notions of what a nation is and what its functions are.

My goals as a traveler have evolved as I've grown into this lifestyle. I've moved away from rapid exploration and set my eyes on settling down somewhere that will match my ideals for at least part of the year on a recurring basis. That search brought me to a town in the valley of southern Ecuador called Vilcabamba, down past the cultural capital of Loja. I was looking for a curated microcosm of sanity in a mostly insane world. Vilcabamba attracted me because of the many positive reports from expatriates, people who had journeyed from all over the world, to seek solace in its peaceful valley.

Vilcabamba is known locally as "El Valle de Lon-gevidad," meaning "The Valley of Longevity." The name is derived from rumors that the inhabitants live statistically long lifespans, with one of the highest con-centrations of centenarians (people over the age of 100) in the world. Areas such as these around the world are called "Blue Zones." Their claims of longevity are attributed to better air, water, and soil, a perennial spring-like climate, and a lifestyle that ne-cessitates low stress and regular exercise.

The town in Vilcabamba is a mix of locals who have lived there for generations and foreigners from dozens of countries who have chosen it as their adopted home. Ecuador has the most open borders of any country in the world, allowing citizens of every coun-try except 12 to enter for up to three months as a tour-ist. Citizens of most other South American nations can enter with an ID card alone. They are even one of a handful of nations who recognize the validity of the politically independent World Passport. The result is a refreshing blend of world cultures. Contrast this with a nation like Turkmenistan, which bars all interna-tional visitors from entering unless they acquire a 10-day tourist visa in their home country.

Ecuador, the most biodiverse country per area in the world, attracts people who value immersion into different climates and ecosystems. It has become a re-tirement haven for Americans, similar to Costa Rica 20 or 30 years prior, but without becoming overrun. The slow pace of life and lush natural surroundings made me feel like I was living as a functioning part of my environment. As an expat, I was mostly left alone, free to make my own choices about how I would spend my time. I could hide away from the world in the trees or just as easily spend my days meeting interesting characters in the shops and cafes.

When I stumbled onto Vilcabamba, I was on a quest to find the place I could call my home, both for now and the indefinite future. It was going to be a place where I could raise my future children away from the prying eyes and aggressive expectations of modern culture. I was so impressed with Vilcabamba's unique combination of elements that I purchased an acre of land with the intention of returning to build a home when the time was right. I haven't yet found anywhere else quite like it, though I will never close my eyes to the possibility.

As much as I like some of the places I have been, each has its unique merits and downfalls. That is why it is unlikely that I will ever stay in one place full time. I would prefer to live a multicultural lifestyle that will give my family access to the best of what the world can offer, according to our subjective values and needs. I can make these choices because I have worked hard to discover who I am and how that fits in with the world. Whatever your starting conditions, you owe it to yourself to find the places that will enable you to live your life as who you are.

A person with awareness of both themselves and the world must determine which cultural conditions are most in line with who they are and what they care about. The answer for me so far has been predominantly Latin America. Nowhere else in the world has given me the same slow pace of life, ideal year-round climate, immersion with nature, and welcoming attitude. The rock-bottom cost of living is just the cherry on top. However, I know other suitable options will emerge in the years of exploration to come.

Where will you find your own personal lifestyle haven? You won't know until you look. You must first understand yourself well enough to know what to look for. The answer to what you want may surprise you, as will the reality of being in a place long-term. It takes time to lose the eyes of novelty and cease feeling like a tourist. That's when you start to live as a part of their world.

It's tempting to copy what others have already found success with – but following in their footsteps because they have proven that it can be done will not be in service to your unique identity. You will be just trading one cultural script for another. I caution anyone who considers taking up the mantle of a global explorer from falling into this convenient trap. Tourist mentality is a form of willing self-delusion. The unadvertised truth about many popular travel destinations is that they are only enjoyable for a few weeks or months at a time. They offer the lifestyle equivalent of a rich dessert at the end of a boring meal. Those first few bites are amazing, but if it's all you ever eat you will become dulled to its overwhelming attributes. You start to long for something else because it's not a sustainable form of enjoyment. You cannot make a sound lifestyle decision based on the excitement of new opportunity. Those are the conditions that lead a lonely spouse to find a new lover or a deprived college student to drink his boredom away.

When you finally have the freedom to do what you want, how long do you remain carefree in that attitude before you do something meaningful with your life again? To go from no freedom to complete freedom is a dangerous thing for a mind that has not yet learned its own wants and limits. A patient person knows to go slowly, so as not to be fooled by novelty. There is no single right way to do this. Every place offers strengths and weaknesses through its laws, geography, and cultural values. Because I have lived in some of the poorest and wealthiest parts of the world, I have a deeper perspective on the spectrum of human life than most. It keeps me perpetually appreciative of what I have but always striving for more. Those who have only ever known total poverty or total prosperity never seek anything outside their narrow window on life.

My favorite parts of the world are the ones in a state of rapid development from poverty to prosperity. They are economically developed enough to offer basic comforts but haven't lost the authenticity that comes from people who struggle to get by. They are grateful for what they have but seem to have adopted the ambition to reach for something more. The younger generations are willing to improve themselves and apply their new talents to their surroundings. That's the innovative spirit of the human race I think we lose as we become too comfortable. We must, at some point, suffer to discover ourselves completely. It's these in-between places (which some people have referred to as "second world" countries) where I feel most at home. They aren't always easy to find. It's often either one extreme or the other.

The Republic of Georgia (often confused with the U.S. state sharing its name) has earned a special place in my heart as one of these surprise transitional gems. Most educated people speak at least conversational English. You can take a train or shared taxi to almost anywhere in the country in just a few hours for a few dollars. There's a strong cafe and restaurant culture with a variety of inexpensive world food options. A Westerner could enjoy a modern, comfortable existence on $500 a month or less in Georgia. It is also the type of place where both the people and the government seem to appreciate the presence of tourists and expatriates. Such an inviting attitude is vitally important if one's goal is to live among the people, not above them. There are many places I've attempted to establish roots where I was treated like an unwelcome guest on both public and private levels. That's never been the case with Georgia. Officials have minimized the bureaucratic runaround for starting a business, opening a bank account, or acquiring five-year residency. In a telling border policy, citizens of most countries can even stay up to 360 days a year as a tourist, and anyone can apply to become a Georgian citizen by presidential decree any time they want.

To me, these are the hallmarks of a nation that welcomes knowledge, resources, and innovation with open arms. It paves the way for a promising future if they can maintain these progressive policies. They are the indicators I look for when deciding whether a country has the long-term potential to match my lifestyle preferences and strategic planning. They are many of the reasons I chose Ecuador as a place to put down roots. In the future, I'd like to take the time to dive deeper into the continent of Africa and see what hidden gems conventional travel wisdom overlooks.

My required comforts are basic now. I don't want to have to worry about the internet, hot water, or power shutting off. I don't want to be treated like a sideshow attraction or an easy target for mooching and theft. I don't appreciate excessive noise, and I don't want to get sick if I eat the local food (which, to date, has only happened in India). I'm also not a fan of cold winters. If I can find a place that embodies these traits and doesn't cost me an arm and a leg to live, I know I will have found somewhere special indeed.

My strategy is tailored to my needs. It will not fit what others require to express themselves to the fullest. The grass always seems greener on the other side, and there's no reason you must settle for just one home base. People start thinking about what is going on in Asia or Europe when they are in Latin America too long or vice versa. You could rent an apartment in one place, own a home in another, or set up enough connections on the ground in each of your favorite places so you always have somewhere to stay. If your home bases are near major airports, you will always have an easy way to move between them. You may choose to spend your summers in Europe when the weather is warmest or leave to avoid a rush of sun-seeking tourists.

I don't have a base of operations in Asia yet, but if I ever do it is likely to be in the Philippines, which I have referred to often as "the poor man's Hawaii." The Philippine islands have many of the traits I love: perpetual beach weather, a low cost of living outside the major cities, immersion with nature, and locals who speak English and are welcoming to foreigners. It and East Timor have the distinction of being the only Christian countries in East Asia. In many ways, the Philippines is the most "western" part of the East.

In the Philippines, I would even have easy access to fresh durian – a large, spiky, tropical fruit that smells like vomit and tastes like heaven.

For many travelers, the multiple home base strategy is the most comfortable way to see the world and never get bored with any single place. It is far more affordable than booking hotels and short rentals everywhere. You can pick and choose a variety of lifestyles from big city to small town, rainforest, white sand beach, mountain village, or anything in between. It's also the best way to acquire second residence permits and citizenship, depending on the requirements of the country.

Lifestyle arbitrage makes it possible to earn a living in a country where wages are high and business is good, but spend it where the cost of living is considerably lower. It is common in America for people to live just outside major cities, where the rent is low, commuting daily to the center, where wages are high. The same principle can be applied on an international scale. The internet now makes commuting all but obsolete for many types of work. Today, people can run their businesses or work for employers based in New York or London while they live in a charming pueblo of Mexico or along a pristine beach in Thailand.

When you free yourself from the chains of your past, you don't have to keep repeating the same limiting patterns any longer. The point is to give up the arbitrary allegiance you have for where you came from.

Learn to look at what the world offers from neutral eyes. Go where you are celebrated, not tolerated. It is only when you find harmony between who you are and what is going on around you that you can begin a true integration with the world.

PART 8

Return to Ordinary

Making Peace with the Past

No matter where you go in the world, no matter what changes you witness in your environment... there will always be something unspoken that you carry with you. Everything you ever experience, no matter how new and unconventional it seems, is colored by the rules you learned in the past about how things work. Your early past tells you what to pay attention to and the values you should hold. It is your primordial culture, and many people mistakenly believe it to be fixed for life.

To abandon the narrative convenience of your culture means to isolate yourself, to an extent, from your peers. Conventional desires won't appeal to you anymore. Something else will have to take their place. Your personal culture goes much deeper than the place you grew up and the rules that society taught you. It's your own version of history – a story almost everyone takes for granted as true.

I understand now why it was impossible for me to go back to my old life. I also know why it was impossible for the influences of that life to come with me to the new one. There was no reference for the path I was on. I watched them get snatched up, one by one, by the overwhelming influence of their culture, hardening themselves into part of a larger group identity in which I had no place. I realized then that people can only learn whatever fits their existing presuppositions. New ideas must match what they are prepared to consider. Opening the mind to new possibilities is painful. Removing old, deeply rooted ideas is psychologically damaging.

These mental limits form the invisible barriers to our actions. They are the unseen cage in which we are all confined. We cannot function outside of the collective truth of a group identity to validate us, affirming the conclusions we think we have reached on our own. When we stop pushing those limits, we will only grow narrower in our working paradigm of who we are and what we can accomplish in the world. Those who realize this must rise above collective limitation to arrive at the center of themselves.

When most people speak of an open mind, they mean the willingness to include new information in their worldview. It's much harder to reassess what they already believe, to erase what is already there. To deconstruct what one considers to be an immutable part of themselves is difficult. It's a painful process of immolation, akin to psychological suicide. The seeker must be willing to bear the pain of the process for the sake of learning the truth about themselves.

This is about so much more than just exploring new parts of the world or ways of living. It is about seeing familiar things in a new way. You can invert exploration to cover the places you came from. Apply what you have learned by immersing yourself into the unknown of your old self. Then you will see what you still cling to, despite all your apparent outward progress.

Transformation is not just a broad new future. It is a reconsidered past. The two are intimately connected. Your past is where you picked up the obstacles that show up regularly in your life now. No matter what new places you go, you carry these familiar obstacles with you. The present moment is built on everything that came before it, a story that only you retell. You are the only author who can rewrite its unconscious influence.

Every traveler knows his experiences in the world influence his identity, but it is much harder for them to see how their perception of new things is biased by what has happened in the past. It's time to delve into your past with the same unhinged curiosity you hold for the world at large. This is a journey into the personal culture of you. You will learn to look at yourself as an unordinary outsider does – a tourist in your own memories. It is a necessary step to understand how and why things came to be the way they are.

Look at the relationships that formed you. The people we interact with during our development influence us. They form our baseline for human interaction. "Family" is just a word for an archetype of bonding and group dynamics in the human psyche. Family is the first micro-society and micro-culture we ever know. It teaches us how to live with other people. Your conception of family, or lack thereof, has influenced your ideas about how to interact with others as friendly, romantic, or authoritative figures.

Like many rebellious young boys, I was never close to my parents during my upbringing. Even in childhood, I saw my mother and father only as the enforcers of limitation to my growth. I believed I was sacrificing my potential for the sake of their conceptions of normality. This oppressive view extended naturally to my teachers, law enforcement, politicians, and anyone who held a limiting role over my life. It was an unshakeable part of my personal narrative, and it had a profound effect on my actions.

I took that familiar narrative with me as I made my way to places strange and unknown. It gave me my operating instructions for how to deal with many of the people I met in the early parts of my journey. There were similar templates in place for my interactions with pretty girls, social competitors, and every other category in my social hierarchy. To change how I interacted with the world, I needed to undo those outlines.

When I returned to San Diego from my first trip abroad in Costa Rica, I learned that my mother and father were about to be divorced after 27 years of marriage. This news was as much a shock to mother as it was to her children. Her entire sense of identity was upturned with one inconvenient disclosure. A simple and sudden change destroyed her unassailable truths. The person she thought she was no longer existed, and the forced realization of that fact was destroying her. She cried herself to sleep alone, every night for months.

Everyone in my mother's life consoled her with promises that things would eventually go back to normal. Her hope in this dark time rested in the idea that she would eventually be able to resume the life she had always known, minus one husband. Because I had distanced myself from my parents many years prior, I held no attachment to my mother's narrative as my father's wife. I was in a unique position to look at her with new eyes, as an unknown woman grieving the loss of her old life. She ceased to be "my mother," the character in my old narrative. In her vulnerability, I saw a human side of her I had no previous association with. Due to my exploratory experiences of myself in

Costa Rica, I was able to let go of my negative formative memories of her to get to explore this new information.

My mother and I were each at a point of emptiness in our lives. That is what enabled us to change the established canon of our relationship. We could meet anew, as if for the first time, as complete strangers sharing no history. That mutual loss of past narratives is the reason my mother and I share a healthy relationship to this day. She too no longer has to treat me as her young, rebellious son. None of that would have been possible if we had both stayed trapped in the former interpretations of who we were. We had to be willing to forget our assumptions about each other and ourselves.

We were all once dependent upon our family archetypes for survival. That's why they hold such important places in our minds throughout life. But we can move beyond our feeble starting conditions and learn to take care of ourselves without that family structure. We don't need to recreate it anymore to function. People who cannot re-examine their past never complete this transition into psychological adulthood. Until they can remove the offending associations from where they started, there will always be a cap to how far they can go. They will relive those untimely events, no matter what changes occur around them.

People who travel to run away from their old life never get very far. Sure, they can get on a plane and be thousands of miles away in just hours. But they cannot so easily alter the conditions their old world instilled into them. They carry their culture with them wherever they go, repeating its effects abroad. They bring their past into the present, shaping the trajectory of their future. Overcoming the culture of your home country isn't enough. You must free yourself from your own history – or forever remain a prisoner of who your early influences told you to be. It is the DNA of your recurring experience.

This is the hardest step for most. Even when we grow beyond patriotism and the need for a country to call home, we still hold the past as sacred. It is what gives us our ultimate sense of self. It is the thing we are most terrified to lose. We don't know what we are without it, in the same way that a prisoner, when locked away for long enough, will forget what life looks like outside the limitations of his cell. The space between the death of the old and the birth of the new is the final frontier for everyone.

No one can change past events. What needs changing is the constant reinterpretation of those events. People are so obsessed with what has happened to them they cannot tell the difference between the actual event and their recollection. When you tell the story of you, you pick apart the tiniest details from every possible moment that has contributed to your present being. You tell the history of how things came to be. Who would you be right now, in this moment, if you were to forget that story? How much of you is only there because of the things you continue to tell yourself about who you are? Whatever remains true once you strip away all the inherited behaviors is what truly defines you. It's also the only way to find out what you want from your existence.

It seems such a simple thing to be aware of what one wants. Yet, we are pulled toward opposing goals all the time. There is no core identity – no defining principle to guide our actions into a non-contradictory state of living. A person comes to know who they are by abandoning the labels they cling to. Then they can act without interference from the past. Even in the clarity of a new environment, commitments from the past persist until the individual chooses what to focus on. Such a person is compelled toward bigger ideals, free from the bonds of their imprisoned past.

When you rise above the constraints of your past, you accept that every choice you make is in your own hands. You are free to do whatever you want, whenever you want, without the forces of former influence to constrain you. You can abandon your career or your family. You can start a conversation with someone new. You can get on a plane to the other side of the world. Or you can do nothing at all. Accepting this burden of choice makes everything you do utterly more profound. Out of everything you could potentially be doing, you are choosing to read this book instead of another. Later, you will choose to drink a glass of water instead of whiskey. Perhaps you will choose to go to work tomorrow, instead of choosing to quit. The responsibility of each moment of your life rests on your shoulders. True adulthood begins the moment you take accountability for your own thoughts and actions.

Someone who values their own existence does not wait for circumstances to change. They are doing whatever they can in each moment – no matter the environment – to express the fundamental values that define them. To operate as oneself is to create a specific type of change in the pursuit of satisfaction. Armed with that principle, every day is a chance to grow the scale of its implementation. The higher your self-worth, the more you will leverage your existence to acquire what you want.

I've been back to my home of San Diego several times since leaving. There is now only the recollection of a place I came from and the recognition that I do not belong there. It is not my home anymore. It seems alien and weird to the person I am now, even though for most of my life it was all I knew. It was the outer threshold that contained my expanding self for 18 years. As you branch out into the world, you'll return to places you visited earlier in your journey, but they won't seem the same. Their influence on you will be different because you will be at a different place internally. I've also been back to Costa Rica a few times over the last decade. While it's still enjoyable and holds a special place in my heart, it will never have quite the same magical effect on me it did during that initial year of exploration.

Every year now, I look back on what I was doing at the same time 12 months before – consistently amazed at how much my circumstances have changed, how many new experiences I've had, and how much I have grown. People who live the same life every day never get this grand perspective on the subtle changes in their identity. New perspective is a humbling experience. People tend to accept that whatever information they hold is the limit to what they can hold. Perpetual novelty forces them to realize the truth.

This is the time when you are capable of asking the questions that will alter the way you understand yourself and interact with the world. It is why only the deeply desperate ever find the answers they seek. Others are content to repeat the same cycles and solve the same problems throughout their lives. What will it take to dislodge yourself from your comfortable sense of identity? Sooner or later, something will happen to give you the space to reconsider your past. When it does, you must be willing to step outside your old interpretations of your life. Neutrality is a blessing. It is the light that wipes away outdated associations, making room for something unknowably superior.

The people we saw ourselves as before other people started telling us who we are is not lost forever. Many philosophies throughout history have encouraged the practice of meditation or other cleansing rituals to rid the mind of junk associations it picks up along the path of life. I prefer a somewhat more hands-on approach. Through questioning, it is possible to undo the ideas one holds – regardless of how long they have been in place. A dedicated mind can trace any idea backward in epistemology, figuring out where it came from and why it has persisted so long. You must be willing to answer the question of why you believe what you believe. It will be difficult to go this far back with your most cherished beliefs, as they tend to be your earliest.

Only when you've found something irreducible in its complexity can you rest. Those are the core axioms that make up everything else about you. They have nothing to do with where you are from or the things you were taught growing up. Teachings can only remind us of what already exists in one's identity, activating a certain awareness and enabling greater actions. It's about forgetting who you think you are and discovering what was there before anything else.

To spend your life as anything other than what you are is madness. It's the madness that leads to the multitude of social problems forever plaguing our world – things like war, poverty, crimes, and slavery in all its forms. To save yourself and our world, you only need to abandon the chaotic thinking of culture that has led us astray for so long. When you are finally free, you will want to stop the spread of this madness any further. The cycle begins again with every new generation, and your children will be no exception if you don't change things now.

PART 9

Integration with the World

Your Role in the Narrative of Life

My goal from the start of this journey has been to impart to you the motivation to undertake a monumental transformation. You may find help along the way from others who are further along or challenge you to grow through the effects of their existence. But it is a path that must be ventured alone. You must dive into isolation before you can emerge victorious over yourself.

The journey is at once timelessly identical and utterly unique for each person. It begins anew in every person who develops awareness of the longing. Each person takes the first steps in their own way. Most drop off at some convenient detour along the way, finding temporary comfort in one of life's many distractions. For some, the journey starts due to a sublime accident. Happenstance pushes them past their breaking point. From that moment, their fate is sealed. They have left the orbit of their old life and may never return.

Beginning the journey is easy. Recognizing its conclusion is much more elusive. There is no finish line to cross and no contest to win. The game stays in play as long as you exist. People cannot accept that there is no big end to personal development. They lust after some perfect state of enlightenment, which is a fictional characteristic we project when we need a hero to look up to, no matter how high we ascend. The concept of enlightenment prevents us from ever mastering our inherited limitations. Instead, we should aspire to become ideal forces for our authentic values through our actions.

Knowing your place in the world is more than knowing the physical location where you belong. It is knowing how you will operate as an interactive part of the world. It describes your job, relationships, hobbies, and charitable pastimes. Every action you take is a change you bring to the world. You can create change without function, only in reaction to events until the time you expire. Or you can choose the change you will stand for, shaping your environment in its image.

Those who never undertake the journey remain forever stuck in their madness, eternally divided against themselves. They adopt countless ways to seek higher purpose, but will live their whole lives never feeling they got to do what they wanted. How could they? They don't know themselves enough to know what that is. Each of us seeks a larger purpose outside of ourselves when our momentary needs are satisfied. Few have the wherewithal to follow that thread to its end.

When you've figured out your role, you've got the difficult task of expressing it as congruent with the cultures of the world. You've got to take what is valuable to you and find a place for it in the hearts of others. Think of all the things you have done for no other reason than they gave you a sense of fulfillment. Deeply imagine what you would spend your time doing if you never had to do anything at all. You must be brave enough to answer why you don't spend all your time doing that. An honest answer now will set the trajectory for the rest of your life.

The fallback answer is that it's impossible to make room for what you want to do because too many problems burden you. The real answer is that you have inherited cultural limitations on what you can do with your time. You can't do the things you want because the world hasn't permitted you. Just as the barriers to travel are now psychological in their nature, the barriers to passion arc the same. The self-aware individual must move beyond these limits to embody the principles that stir their emotions. You will discover what these are when you have explored what remains beyond the old self.

Culture tells us to scorn people who get what they want without breaking their backs along the way. We intuitively hate people who apply their gifts in domains where others do not, as we feel threatened by anyone who sets big goals for themselves. So long as a person believes it is beyond their control to improve their life, they will vilify men and women of passion. You take a major social risk every time you go against the grain because you threaten the bond of shared identity. The bond can be superficial, such as the way we look. Racial supremacy is born here. It can be incidental, like where we happened to have been born. We call this nationalism. Or it can be ideological, like the values that shape our actions. Those who boldly proclaim what they stand for are a threat to everyone still caught in culture's tendrils.

When you identify yourself by values, you adopt a radical outlook on ordinary things. A profession changes from an economically imposed labor routine to an opportunity to leverage influence. You start working on the things you care about and making money doing what you love. Even if you end up somewhere that appears to be the same as the conventional path, how and why you are there will be unique to you. What is important is the psychological impact of our actions, which is where meaning resides. As the author of your own narrative, your interpretation of how you spend your time will be the only one that matters.

The inversion of culture's influence signals the start of your new life. Instead of culture's victim, you become its creator. Your body will be a mechanism for shifting reality toward the type of world you want to live in. You won't be bound by the impressions the world placed within you. You'll believe what you believe because it is congruent with who you are. You'll structure the activities of your life around what works.

Part of me has always thought that if the world found out what I really was, it would reject me. The people in my life could not be ready for what I saw within myself. I was tempted, for the longest time, to walk away from the human world and remain on my own until I expired. Having already acquired the independence I would need to survive, both physically and spiritually, I had grown comfortable with my existence and did not fear isolation. I saw no way for the person I was becoming to coexist with the world as I perceived it. Similar sentiments have echoed endlessly in the past as individuals have grown aware of themselves.

In my recent past, my ambition changed. Maybe I got stronger. Maybe I became more aware of what the problem was and realized what I could do about it. I reached the conclusion that I had a place somewhere. I would still be something of an outsider – living on the fringe and doing things the way I wanted– but I would not completely abandon the trappings of society. Everything I have seen so far gives me a vantage place from which to plot my involvement in the world. I see better now what people need, and I understand what I am equipped to provide.

I could not accept the easiest role that life would offer me. Gregory Diehl had to be someone I could live with. It was a matter of presenting myself as the type of person the world could accept, but who would still push against the limits of culture. It became a balancing act of staying one step beyond their complacency. Too far would upset them and not far enough would be benign. It took trial and error, experimenting with how the world would respond to different versions of me. There was a type of person in a certain place in their life who would value what I offered. They would seek me out and hold onto me when they found me.

It didn't matter if I couldn't solve the world's larger problems. There was a specific domain where I could affect the way people think and act. That is where I would carve out my role in the narrative of life. Most importantly, I could do so without betraying the principles I now knew defined me. I do not fear that the role I inhabit will lead to my stagnation. People who think they need to live a certain way until death have neutered their potentialities. They will not fare well in a world that accelerates its cultural freedoms.

When I visited Ghana in 2014, I took on the role of teaching entrepreneurship to youths who had traveled to Kumasi to join the annual Liberty & Entrepreneurship Camp, led by the Africa Youth Peace Call. Despite my range of travel experiences, Ghana was a cultural anomaly for me. I'd seen nearly every variant of poverty or instability throughout the other continents I had visited. In Ghana, I got the sense daily power and water shutoffs were accepted without comparison to any known alternative. The Ghanaians were friendly, almost to a fault, but also looked upon me as a source of casual financial handouts. They were not like the muggers and moochers I was used to elsewhere. It was like they held a childlike view of money, as though they had no idea where it came from or why someone who had more than they did might not want to give it away to anyone who asked. Passing along the principles of entrepreneurship was probably the most valuable role I could play so that they could adopt the mentality of productive players in a global economy.

Whatever role I play in the unpredictable future will be true to what I am. I am now aware of what I can do best to co-exist with the world and produce the kinds of influence it needs. The rest I will figure out in the moment. I have earned that improvisational certainty through a lifetime of struggling under different conditions. It has prepared me for an open future where anything can happen, and I can become anyone I must to live out my principles. The person I act as now is the best person I have so far figured out how to be, offering to the world what I perceive it needs and I am best qualified to provide. At the intersection of what you desire to offer and your environment demands is where you will find your role. No one can be all things to all people because you are limited in what you can do and everyone else is limited in their focus.

Everywhere I go in the world, I see broken systems, suffering, and inefficiencies. Because of this heightened awareness, I can choose to care or not. I can act on these observations or ignore them. You have the same awareness over certain domains in your life. You choose every day whether to care and whether to act. Though I have learned to appreciate the good things in every culture, perspective has also made the flaws overwhelmingly obvious. I have a mind honed for seeing mistakes in all things. I see the weaknesses in how people act and the wasted energy in the way a city operates. I notice all the ways people could be living better if they got their act together. I cannot help most of them any more than I could help the Chinese children growing up as prisoners in a utilitarian machine. They do not want my help. They would never consider the possibility or the need.

Every strange experience has shown me a part of myself I could not have come to know any other way. There were countless pieces of me locked away, which I could only intuit from afar. They were unlocked through unique experiences that showed my brain the limits to culture were further out than I thought. The world is a book of many pages, waiting to be read. The self is a library of ancient tomes written in languages you cannot understand. You grow accustomed to the characters you find on the first shelf and never get to read what remains of the vast arena. I am excited by what I may become as I gather my resources, learn new things, and watch the world change.

It doesn't matter that there is no single culture on this planet perfect for what I strive to be. We are moving into a future beyond borders. I am not limited to what convention allows. Explorers arrange the elements of the systems around them in service to their identities. When necessary, they build new systems for what they want. Those who have no place among our species can make their own and become the ideal embodiment of their principles. When you've seen what needs to change in the world, your emotions will give you the strength to act.

Your larger mission will overlap with a segment of the world that needs what you do. No one will have to endure what you cannot abide. You'll work so that no one else will have to survive the pain you know so well. You have survived it. You can handle the fire when others cannot. Your greatest power will be defined by the influence you hold on the space around you. Be brave enough to drive all other goals from your mind.

PART 10

Shape the Future

Owning Your Influence

From the first moment we are conscious of our own existence, we pick up on how the world works. Because we are born feeble, we endow our parents with the burden of preparing us for life as they already know it to be. They show us not just how to survive, but how to be at ease with existence. They pass on what they have learned so we will be able to navigate the world without them. The ideas they implant linger with us throughout life, making their unfinished business our own. They create our culture.

The irony of this sad situation is that independence cannot be taught by someone who has not first obtained it. Emotional maturity cannot be demonstrated by someone who isn't fully self-expressed. Effective instructions for living can't be imparted by people who haven't learned how to live. The unsurprising result is that most of us will become stunted in childhood. We spend the rest of our lives capping our abilities because of developmental influences from our impressionable years. Few are able to use the pain of early years to propel into personal greatness.

For children, no time ever passes without a plan for its occupation. Culture prescribes how every developmental milestone will unfold. By the time children reach adulthood, they've yet to experience a life without instructions. Social demands interrupt the search for one's identity. Paradise, once lost, is rarely found again. Some pick it up a few decades later when they realize something is deeply wrong in their lives. Most die never having lived at all. When growing young people cannot express themselves without restraint, they develop a nagging sense of spiritual emptiness until they die.

We have all had inadequate upbringings because we were not given the tools we would need to discover who we were. We face a crossroads: either learning from the mistakes of the past or repeating them with our own children. The passing of values to the new minds concludes the self-discovery cycle, yet it is the step most often overlooked. Parents and educators have important jobs because they tell us how we should think and what we should believe. Most of them do not realize the importance of their role in human development. We believe what they teach because we have nothing to contrast it. We simply cannot imagine existing any other way, resulting in a population that has no idea what it means to learn of their own accord.

Cultural upbringing ignores the will of the child. It assumes the collective knows what is best for the individual. Group identity overpowers individual awareness throughout its unfolding. Collectivized learning corrals the individual to exist within the limits of their own cultural identity. By restricting diversity in individual learning, we also restrict the depth of the individual. People are prepared for life as functional members of an arbitrary social paradigm that will be replaced with another every generation.

During my first trip to Europe, I was employed by a combination nursery and preschool in Genoa, Italy inspired by the unconventional teaching philosophies of Maria Montessori. Before taking the job, the school director emphasized how different the structure of learning and level of freedom given to the children were compared to conventional schools. Their mission was to give children the opportunity to guide their own learning from the earliest age. They only wanted teachers who embodied this philosophy, which is why they were eager to work with me.

When I arrived in Italy, the childcare reality was starkly different from the picture the director had painted. The children, as young as two years old, had tight schedules for each day with specific hours dedicated to specific activities. Though they told a better story and operated with bigger smiles, I still operated as part of a structure that existed to define how early childhood would be allowed to play out. Even under the most progressive of circumstances, it seemed impossible to escape the limiting effects of schooling institutions in formative years.

Authentic education is how a mind comes into healthy maturity. It is the self moving from futility to power over the span of a lifetime, fueled by passion and curiosity. It cannot be forced without confidence. A mentor needs to ignite this curiosity in young people, inspiring them to explore the fullest capacity of their experience. They are a coach and guide for this personal evolution, overseeing the initial discovery of identity. The immature child is just like a tourist in a foreign country and their guardians are tour guides introducing them to their way of life.

One thing is certain. Everyone raises their children in a world different than the one they were raised in. You cannot prepare them for the challenges they will face using your lessons. Only if they value humility will they meet the demands of perpetual change. This can only happen when parents conquer their allegiance to the dead past. Parents and other mentors must embrace neoteny to become childlike learners again, questioning everything they thought to be true. It requires a total allegiance to honesty and the determination to never ignore new information that invalidates cherished beliefs. They must hold the innate curiosity lost as we grow too comfortable.

To influence another life is to invest a part of yourself into the identity into someone else. That investment returns daily through the demands learners make upon teachers to encourage them to grow too. Children have much to teach adults, so long as they can view things through their undeveloped eyes. Children can unlock our emotional capacity, which is why immature adults can be so uncomfortable around them. They expose the parts of us we work to hide. Every child is pleading for adults to show them the world is safe to express themselves. Pass on what you have learned without pressure so that they may find their own identities.

The fallacy of influencers is they believe it is their job to implant others' minds with the same ideas they have come to believe over the course of their journey. Such an attitude is the enemy of progress. Everyone begins the journey anew in a different time and under different externalities. Some will take up the mantle where you left off – but it will not be exactly the same. Adaptation means solving today's problems today and laying the ground for whatever tomorrow's problems may be. If we cannot get out of the way, we will replicate only the problems we are prepared to solve.

Those who are secure in their own identity do not need to force it on others. Everyone naturally wants to share their values with those who will listen, but only broken people try to turn others into copies of themselves. When you take on a leadership role, you help others become who they are, not to become more like what you have discovered yourself to be. That is the reason I cannot tell you that travel is the path to the transformation you need. That it was my ideal path has no bearing on you. You must discover this for yourself. Arbitrary importance given to yourself is a form of subtle narcissism. The final battle, and the one so many people come so far just to lose, is getting over yourself. You are, in one sense, the most important thing in the universe and also utterly insignificant. When you can accept these dual truths, you will be ready to take the world where it needs to be, in its own way and time.

The details of how you will accomplish this hardly matter. They will be different for each person's abilities and environment. We all must figure out what we are suited to do through our unique experiences. We can all help other people break free from the barriers of culture in some way. My path showed me that my greatest assets would be my ability to communicate important information and persuade people to attempt new things. I foresaw that I would spend my life exploring the possible outlets to that happen. The way you create influence will be a product of what you are. You can stand proudly in front of the world, ready for them to accept or reject you as you are.

Everything a person ever does is in service to their conception of self. Therefore, you can only introduce ideas that the people in your life are ready to hear. The listener must want to receive your offering. Maybe you have an idea of the lessons you are trying to spread, but don't know how to make them heard in a noisy world. You can't always see how to be unique and impactful without sacrificing your authentic identity. The people who scorn or ignore you may be the ones who need your influence the most. The only point of leaving your home behind is to become a human being worthy of living in the world. By doing so, you also make the world worth living in. That is how you move past humanity's great struggle against itself so you may live to see where the story goes. There's a scale model of society's ills playing out in the theater of your mind right now. Solve the riddle of your delusion about who you are and what you stand for.

The world at first rejects whatever does not belong within its molds. But, in time, it will respect anyone who stands firm and proud in front of it as themselves. The world places such people into a category unto themselves – a landmark for what others can become. Observers will unconsciously emulate you because your existence shows them new limits to what is possible. In everything it touches, your influence will bring a little more order into the universe. In the end, you either become someone worth living as or you never really live at all.

This is my hope as you depart from my words – that you will take the lessons here and run them through the laboratory of your own life. A principle applied under different conditions produces unlimited results, none more complete than the last. Every new life is a chance to try again, each identity a different method. Every act is a signal put out for others to receive and interpret. Persist long enough, and you will attract the people who need your influence to move on from the obstacles they hold. It's a reciprocal bond enabling each party to expose greater parts of the whole. Culture is not the enemy when it creates growth for the individuals who compose it. It evolves with us as an ally against the unknown trials of tomorrow. We each grow stronger the more we merge with other people who share our journey. They challenge and encourage us. The independent individual accepts their place in the larger narrative, sending and receiving what is necessary to create growth for everyone.

One day, nations will not be made by yesterday's inherited barriers. They will be forged organically through shared ideals and mutual aid. Family will mean more than the circumstances of one's birth and earliest associations. With influence, you become a beacon for others like you or whose identities complement your own. You begin to see beyond your limits to form unique social structures based on shared goals and values. You become far more than what you could ever be on your own, but only if you are brave enough to communicate your needs and take on others' pain.

The world needs the real you, and you just might need to experience the world to become that. Now go.

Epilogue

You leave the security of your old life without a plan or a path.

Many would encourage anyone to wantonly abandon their old life in pursuit of personal renaissance. This is not the way to freedom. Travel is just one of many possible catalysts that may accelerate the path to liberation.

Any plan belongs to someone else. It cannot be your own.

Your path will not be the same as others. Only introspection can show you which parts of the past you are ready to dismantle. Only curiosity can point you in the right direction. Travelers use everything the world offers to find their identity.

If you do not create the path as you go, you will not arrive at yourself.

Do not wait for things to change. Cast yourself headstrong and willing into uncertainty. Do whatever is difficult until it is no longer difficult. Let yourself grow into all the ways you are capable of being.

Break the rules of culture. Become what you are.

Gregory Diehl is the author of multiple Amazon best-selling books on identity development for businesses and individuals. He is also the founder of Identity Publications, an organization that produces and publishes meaningful books containing ideas that matter. Diehl travels to more than 50 countries, enjoys homesteading the valley of Ecuador, and kidnaps felines from streets around the world.

Listen to his podcast, Uncomfortable Conversations With Gregory, or email him at: contact@gregorydiehl.net.

ACKNOWLEDGEMENTS

Every message of substance must pass through layers of refinement before it is ready for the public eye. My appreciation goes out to a group of advance readers of *Travel As Transformation*, who picked out parts of my premature work that were not communicating things correctly. The feedback they gave enabled me to determine what kind of person would derive the most from my story. Thank you dearly, Chris Backe, Rebecca Cable, Greg Curtin, Kevin Hoelschi, Maria McMahon, JC Mitchell, John Spence, Jackson Sullivan, and Daniel Walvin.

Although each path is unique to the explorer, there are sometimes others who can show us things we would have had difficulty seeing on our own. One such wanderer for me is the great and powerful Helena Lind, whose influence continues to affect my personal and professional development. Here's hoping that someday we might yet share three-dimensional space with each other and our cats.

CAN'T TRAVEL BUT WANT TO HAVE TRANSFORMATION?

Work directly with Gregory Diehl for the growth of your identity. Apply for an exploratory coaching session at: www.gregorydiehl.net/coaching.

During this session, you and Gregory will discuss your reasons for seeking personal development guidance, what you expect to get out of it, and why you chose Gregory for this process of change.

Not everyone is a good fit, but those that are will receive a level of personal development deeper than any they have ever known.

Stop delaying your departure.
Buy the ticket.
Get on the plane.

Come see where unique and meaningful ideas live.

Like Identity Publications on
Facebook.com/identitypublications

Follow Identity Publications on
Twitter.com/identitypublic

Subscribe to Identity Publications on
Youtube.com/c/identitypublications

Find out more about our publishing approach at
IdentityPublications.com

Lightning Source UK Ltd.
Milton Keynes UK
UKHW040626040620
364384UK00003B/792